Building Healthy Friendships

Teaching Friendship Skills to Young People

TERRY BECK

R&E Publishers • *Saratoga, California*

R & E Publishers
P.O. Box 2008, Saratoga, CA 95070
Tel: (408) 866-6303   Fax: (408) 866-0825

Book Design by Diane Parker
Cover illustration Clyde Carver III

Beck, Terry (Terry A.)
    Building healthy friendships: teaching friendship skills to young people / Terry Beck.
        p.   cm.
    Includes bibliographical references.
    ISBN 1-56875-073-0
    1. Friendship. 2. Friendship in children. 3. Friendship--Studying and teaching. 4. Child rearing. I. Title.
    BF575.F66B43 1994
    158'.25--dc20   94-1691
                                                             CIP

Author's Note

Using true stories and anecdotes to illustrate and clarify friendship skills is my favorite form of teaching. However, on the written page introducing new people with every vignette quickly overwhelms the reader's ability to identify with familiar characters. For the sake of smooth reading and simplicity, I have taken the liberty of compiling the experiences of many young people and adults and assigning them to a set group of people. In very simple terms that means that, although these stories have happened, they may not have happened to the individuals mentioned in the book in exactly the way they are related.

Dedication

To...

...my parents, Louis and Ruth Allen, who taught their children the skills of friendship at an early age, and offered vast amounts of encouragement and technical advice in the writing of this book;

...my sister, Deborah, my first forever friend, who taught me the meaning of expressing myself through writing;

...my brothers, Michael, Ace, and Steven, whose presence in this book and in my life has been a precious treasure;

...my husband, Randy, whose patient love and support blesses all my endeavors;

...my children, Keidi, Nathan, Laurel, Jordan, Benjamin and Amanda—you are wonderful and I cherish you with all that I am;

...and our Godchildren, Arwen, Franchesca, Dominica, Helen, Felicia, Emily, Hannah, Theresa, Sarah-Anne, Colby, James and our heavenly messenger, Jonathon, with love.

Acknowledgments

With love and gratitude I thank...

...that special group of friends who smoothed the process of writing and publishing this book with their enthusiasm and support—Donna Oberstein, Carol Heacock, Sharon Allen, Margaret Cordrey, Susan Schaaf, Laura Larson, Marilyn Miller, Michelle Peabody, Ruth Duterte, Alisa Roberts, Joanne Vazquez, Eloise Mousalam, Wendy Russell, Kahleen Edeal, Leslie Cooper, Judi Somerville, Kathleen Frey, Ardis Goetz, Geri Mears, Anna Schoepp, Karen Stevens, Cindy Taylor, Linda Maxwell, Diane Lindsay, Barb Christianson, Rebekah Cervantes, Marilyn Nicholas, and Linda Brosamle;

...and the men who assured me that this book was needed by fathers of this land and took time out to share with me their expertise and encouragement, Dan Nicholas, Alan Pagano, Mark Roberts, Fadlo Mousalam, Ron Demolar, David Talbott, Fred Miller, Larry Weeden and the Very Rev. Frs. Simeon Berven, Weldon Hardenbrook and Peter Gillquist.

Contents

Preface

Teaching friendship skills became part of my life out of necessity. Giving birth to six children did not prepare me for parenthood. Neither did a college degree and courses in child psychology, family relations, and business management. Abnormal Psychology proved helpful, especially on rainy afternoons when all of the children and their friends are playing inside our house.

In Chapter 1 you will meet Harley, and in his story understand where the idea of teaching friendship as specific skills developed. Harley was five when he came to us. He is twenty-two today. In the interim years my interest in making friendship skills a teachable, learnable art led to the development of *The Workshop of Friendship*, a seminar for adults and teens, and now this book.

My ongoing education in working with children comes from hands-on experience, supplemented by professional parenting classes and personal research. Caring for foster children from a wide variety of backgrounds for periods ranging from one week to five years, raising our family, teaching at a preschool, and running a community recreation program has been the core of my experience. From this, I dare to share what I am learning.

Experience has shown that learning friendship skills and using them is not enough to ensure lasting relationships. There are times when I go through the motions of friendship without a sincere interest or love for the person with whom I'm relating. In these instances I think of myself as a *friendship mechanic*. My terminology is based on the following word picture which describes improperly fueled friendships.

"You are the proud owner of a sparkling new gas-powered automobile. Having just finished Driver's Training classes and received a driver's license, you feel competent to handle this prized possession in all circumstances. Your first step as a new owner is to fill the car with fuel. Unfortunately, instead of filling the car with gas, you fill it with diesel fuel.

For a time, the car operates somewhat normally. Huge billows of white smoke follow the car around town and its power on hills is discouraging, but at least you get where you're going. As time passes, the car becomes less dependable. Eventually the diesel fuel freezes the engine, and the car stops running altogether. Your beloved automobile, still shiny and beautiful, sits alone and abandoned in the driveway."

Humans are made to run on only one fuel: divine love. They do not function well on any thing else. We can go through the motions of friendship without love. Like the car filled with diesel fuel, we may appear to be operating normally, at least temporarily. But to get lasting joy out of our vehicle and our friendships, we must use God's love to power them.

The condition of our vehicle or the road our lives will travel does not end with the final pages of this book; for you or for me. Learning to love in friendship is a process, as is forgiveness, courtesy, kindness, giving, loyalty, and the other skills presented in this book. We will probably encounter everything from flat tires to fender-benders as we travel the freeways and country roads of friendship. Whatever we do, the first step is to begin by trusting God to control the attitudes of our hearts and the direction of our journey. Then, honing our skills with knowledge and practice and powered by the right fuel, we are able to offer the blessing of friendship. In turn, we will be blessed with that joy ourselves.

A carpenter with no tools is no carpenter.
--Midrash

Teaching Friendship: How Can It Be Done?

By Learning Specific Skills. . .

When five year old Harley came to live with us, he brought nothing but the clothes on his back. His parents were in a drug rehabilitation center. Home was a 1966 Chevy.

To Harley, our comfortable house was a foreign country. The noise of the vacuum cleaner sent him into hiding. He refused to sleep between clean sheets for fear of "wrinkling up their softness." Toys were miracles. Harley fondled a two dollar set of paints for days before allowing himself to use them. Baths were torture: he'd seen a movie about a monster that slithered through water spouts, grabbed children in its mouth, and carried them off through drain pipes.

While we introduced Harley step by step to our world, he brought his world to us. On our first outing to an amusement park, my husband Randy found Harley cheerfully panhandling in the men's room. Money disappeared from my purse and Randy's wallet. Every morning for two weeks Harley was suspended from school for obscene language or indecent exposure.

As troubling as we found these problems, they were minor compared to helping Harley learn to make friends.

"I'll get it!" yelled Harley, responding happily to a knock on our door.

"Hi, I'm Keith. What's your name?" announced the neighbor's little boy. "I live in that brown house. My Mom told me to come and meet you."

"Did you bring me anything?" Harley inquired.

"No." Keith replied.

"D'you want something from me?" Harley asked.

"No." Keith replied again.

"Then get your ugly face out of here! This is my house and I don't want you in it!" The door slammed.

Keith persisted in visiting Harley, to his peril. One morning I noticed Keith limping home across our yard. Harley had kicked him between the legs. What happened?

"That dumb Keith told me I was bossy," said Harley, "I showed him!"

Randy and I were shocked by Harley's behavior. We tried to get him to change. Our local librarian found stories about children's friendships for us to read to him. We asked Harley what he would do to solve the problems the characters encountered. His solutions were cruel or violent.

Trying to anticipate problems was only partly successful. We could never keep up with Harley's imagination. He enticed a little girl into a game of "barber" and chopped off her ponytails with his kindergarten scissors. He ruined his own sixth birthday party by insisting on playing with the new toys and eating the cake alone.

As we dealt with neighbor's complaints and our continuing frustration, we realized we'd have to start at bedrock to show this difficult but endearing savage the value and skills of friendship.

"It's obvious," I announced to Randy after an exhausting day, "Since the school does not offer *Friendship 1A: The Absolute Rockbottom Basics*, we'll have to develop a special class for Harley."

"Good idea," Randy replied seriously to my intended joke. "That may be our best bet. Let's give it a try."

And try we did. We acted out friendship roles with Harley to give him experience and practice using unfamiliar skills. "How would you feel in that person's shoes? How would you want to be treated?" was our constant question to him. We assured him that learning to make friends would bring happiness.

Change came slowly. We reminded Harley (and each other) that learning friendship skills is not achieved all at once; it is a process. Harley finally shared his paints with Keith. When Keith didn't return the brush Harley wanted fast enough Harley bit him.

One day it happened. Keith was crying because Harley made fun of his plywood sword. Harley watched his friend cry for a moment. A look of tenderness crossed his face. He solemnly offered Keith a cookie. I cried.

"Look, Terry, look!" he hollered one day as he climbed out of the school bus. "The teacher gave me a special award and told me to be sure you saw it!"

Bursting with pride, Harley pointed to a large ribbon which stated: *OUTSTANDING STUDENT AWARD* WAS GIVEN TO HARLEY FOR PLAYING WELL WITH HIS CLASSMATES ALL DAY.

. . . And by Personal Demonstration

As we focused on helping Harley learn specific friendship skills, we were delighted to discover that these skills really can be taught to those who are willing to change, including parents. My six children continue to teach me that the *most* effective way to teach friendship skills is by personal example.

While driving our children (ages 5-16) to school one morning, I overheard them discussing a teacher who'd asked her pupils to obey certain rules but who chronically disobeyed those rules herself. They asked me how I felt about the teacher's actions.

I launched into a mini-sermon on the inconsistency of people who are talkers but not doers. Loftily I tossed out statements like "words without actions will condemn them" and "nothing speaks louder to others than the example we offer in our own lives." As an afterthought I asked the children if *I* ever asked them to "do what I said and not what I do." Their response was distressingly immediate.

"You ask us to leave you notes telling you where we're going," commented one. "But you don't leave us notes when you're going out."

"You gripe when we leave dishes in our rooms or on the coffee table, but we find your mugs all over the house," chimed in another.

"When we gossip about our friends on the phone you warn us of the evils of gossip. But you talk to your friends about us and about other people's behavior too."

"You hate it when we get sarcastic with each other, but when you get mad at us, your words drip with sarcasm!" my oldest son announced.

The children's list of my failings went on. Everything they mentioned was true. I was ashamed of myself.

After apologizing for being a poor example of what I was trying to teach them, I borrowed a line from a Sesame Street book. Grover, a fuzzy blue creature of undetermined species, spends the entire book trying to stop the reader from turning pages because, he informs us over and over, "There's a monster at the end of this book!" When it is finally revealed that Grover himself is the monster, he confesses in a very small voice:

"Oh, I am *so* embarrassed!"

Building Friendships Takes Skills

Imagine a family, mother, father, sister, brother, sitting on the edge of a large lot with a beautiful view. They have committed themselves to build a house that will provide comfort and shelter. Next to them is a huge pile of materials; lumber, nails, pipes, sheet rock, shingles. Why are they just sitting there and are not busy working on their building? They have a problem. There are no blueprints. There are no tools. Even if they had blueprints or tools, neither parent knows how to use them. Eventually the family arranges the wood into a cave-like structure, nails shingles over the top, and prays that the rains won't come.

On the next block another family has the same task, but these parents brought tools they had been given in childhood to the job. Their knowledge of construction allows them to draw their own blueprints, which result in a sturdy home for the family. The children work alongside their parents. They are learning how to use tools they will need to build their own homes in the future.

People around us, family, neighbors, classmates, friends, are building materials. Our individual personalities and needs are expressed in the design of the blueprints.

The tools are the friendship skills needed to build healthy, enduring relationships. As carpenters use basic tools to build homes, so can we learn to use the basic tools of friendship—friendliness, listening, giving, courtesy, honoring each other in our speech, fairness in our expectations, loyalty, kindness, apologizing, forgiveness, and encouraging each other to wholeness.

Is friendship a skill we can teach our children like hammering and sawing? The answer is yes for those who are willing to learn and change. This book guides parents and young people step-by-step in developing friendship skills that will help equip them for healthy lives.

Does this all sound too mechanical? Does it seem to complicate what should be a simple and natural process? As with many activities that seem easy and effortless, an important portion of the ability to make friends rests on the mastery of specific skills. These skills may seem difficult at first, but in time will become a rewarding habit.

When our daughter Keidi had her learner's permit she was eager to practice driving, but maneuvering on mountain roads in our big van was challenging. One day I observed her sitting hunched over the steering wheel, her knuckles white as she gripped the vinyl padding.

"Relax, Keidi," I suggested. "Driving's supposed to be fun."

"It may be fun for you, Mom," she replied tersely. "And you make it look easy. But these bicyclists we're passing have no idea how lucky they are to be alive and undamaged after I've scraped by them on these narrow bridges!"

She's right. I hardly think about the mechanics of driving now. But I remember my father sitting tight-lipped in the passenger seat when the driver behind us honked at me for stopping at a corner.

"Why's he honking?" I complained. "There's a stop sign on this corner!"

"Yes, there is," Dad agreed. "But he didn't expect you to stop twenty feet before the sign and then creep up to it at one mile an hour!"

How Will We Go About Learning and Teaching These Skills?

Parents of children of any age, including parents-to-be or parents of children under the age of ten, will benefit by first working through these ideas by themselves or with their spouses. Then they will be equipped to work through the four steps educators have developed for teaching skills. They are:

1. *Explanation*—this book explains friendship skills and offers suggestions on how to implement them.

2. *Demonstration*—parents show how to do the skills by utilizing them in their own lives.

3. *Supervision*—children practice the skills on their own under the guidance of the parents.

4. *Practice*—children incorporate the skills into their relationships.

This learning format is used throughout the book and is reinforced by questions and suggested assignments given at the end of the chapters. Suggestions for integrating these skills into daily life will be discussed in Chapter 2.

Building Healthy Friendships: Teaching Friendship Skills to Young People develops skills through three levels of relationships: casual, meaningful, and intimate. The chapters define and demonstrate each skill.

Get To Know Your Children

While you are reading this book, see if you can deepen your relationship with your children on their terms. This can be a challenging task, as the readiness of children to share their experiences varies greatly with individuals. Some children come home from school or play and blurt out detailed reports of their adventures. "Hi! This is what happened to me today. This is how I felt about it. This is what I did about it. Can I have a snack?" Others may come straight to the point: "Can I have a snack?" It takes careful prompting to get them to open up.

This has been true of our oldest son. Nathan came out of my womb as if shot from a pistol and hasn't stopped moving since. When he was small, I required him to sit on my lap for ten minutes every evening. It was the only guarantee of a chance to touch and talk to him individually. And oh, the delight in his voice when bedtime was announced and he could proclaim, "But I haven't had my ten minutes yet!"

Now that Nathan is a teen-ager and too big to sit on my lap, we walk together several evenings a week. Our favorite hike is to the the top of Mount Hermon. From there, looking out at the valleys and mountains around us, life and our relationship seem to fall into a healthy balance. This is where I get to know my son. Not when I'm after him to finish his homework or his chores. Not when I'm asking him to turn down his radio or to stop shooting the rubber bands off his braces into the casserole. He wears bigger shoes than I do now, and will soon be taller. *Carpe diem*, my heart tells me. Seize the day before it's gone forever.

Children wait for parents to give them the clue, "I'm interested in you."

My cousin and his wife wear their Walkmans, tiny radios that are heard through headphones, in the house, on walks, and in the car. The radio programs they listen to block out contact with their children. The children have adapted in their own ways.

The oldest son, a teen-ager, mumbles his plans to his father's back, knowing that his Dad won't hear him over the music being played on the Walkman, and then proceeds to do as he pleases. When he does something his parents don't like, he can reply, "I told you what I was going to do, and you didn't object!" The second son, a sixth grader, uses profanity to shock his parents into responding to him. The first grade girl directly faces everyone she talks to and repeats every question or greeting three times in a loud voice: "Hi, Aunt Terry. HI, Aunt Terry. HI, AUNT TERRY!" The youngest, a pre-schooler, finds that a high-pitched scream accompanied by a romp through the house in his birthday suit usually gets his parents' attention.

"Walkmans," real or symbolic, that keep us from knowing our children need to be worn with caution and consideration. My "Walkman" is books. I become so absorbed in reading that my children are sometimes unheard and ignored. Hobbies, work, television, sports, substance abuse, volunteer activities... all can impair our availability to befriend our children.

Yes, we do need to be friends with our children. Not buddy-buddy friends. Not equal authority friends. Parenting friends. This parenting friendship will develop over the years until our children mature. Then we can drop the *parenting* qualification. Our investment has yielded deep friendships with those who are closest to us.

Remember the saying, "Children spell love T-I-M-E." Take time to know your child!

Working Through the Book With Your Child

Children under the age of ten are intended to learn the skills presented in this book from their parents or those working with them. Their training will be informal and learn-as-you-grow. For young people ages ten and over (ten is an approximate age—readiness will vary with individual children) I suggest reading and discussing together each of the topics presented. Work through the assignments and answer the questions individually, then discuss the answers.

To accomplish meaningful change, plan an uninterrupted private time with each child weekly or twice a week. Since children learn in small bites, daily may be too often. To provide background, read the chapters out loud together and review the discussion questions. Writing the answers will help some children fix the lessons in their mind and encourage reflection as they put the skills into action. Concentrate on learning and applying one skill at a time.

As you see your children using the friendship skills, support their efforts. Don't laugh when they miss the mark—which they will do. I've overheard my children give their friends advice about relationships that seemed to come straight from outer space. For example, a child has told me they spent an hour talking with Friend A about Friend B's gossiping problem. It's easier to recognize the failings of others for them and for us. Patience is vital. Friendship takes practice.

During the initial training period, or first time through the book, hold off on pointing out blunders your children make. These incidents may be used noncritically as examples during the teaching time or at a teachable moment between discussion sessions. Children learn best when they recognize their own mistakes. With your patient help, they will learn to correct misjudgments when or before they happen. Identifying the problem is the first task. Solving the problem comes next.

Ann Ortlund, author of *Children are Wet Cement* says: "Your child is wet cement, and affirmations are the forms to mold him into his future shape." As you go through these lessons with your child, do it gently, humbly, and noncritically.

As a parent, I am learning to admit fault when I inflict a wrong act or word. I often have to ask my children's forgiveness for failing as an example. Although humility is not a strong point of mine, I am trying to model a basic process in friendship: acknowledging mistakes, apologizing, and asking forgiveness.

Other Ways to Use This Book

Along with using this book within families, it can be used successfully in school classes and youth groups. Many people find a team approach helpful. They invite interested individuals to work on and learn the skills together. One team in our area is made up of a mother, an adult son, her two pre-teenagers and their grandfather. This approach works for them because the team has seen the need in their own lives, agreed on the goal, the approach and the schedule they will follow.

The group or team approach has been a particularly effective way to teach youths whose parents are not willing or able to teach them. Many participants have found it effective to work through the book privately, then to review it with the group. Larger groups tend to encourage more general discussion questions; smaller groups are often more specific. Adult Sunday School classes, parenting support groups, and couples groups will also find this book an excellent learning tool.

The material was developed as a workshop for use with church retreats and is currently the curriculum core for seventh to twelfth grade "Life Preparedness" classes in local private schools.

Remember. . .

Learning friendship skills is within the grasp of all who are willing to grow and change. Friendship is a continual process that calls for the best in us and rewards us emotionally, physically, and spiritually throughout our lives.

Let the adventure begin!

*Experience is the best teacher but,
if you can learn from the experience of
others the tuition is less.*

Preparing Ourselves

"I Hate to Admit It, But I'm Drowning!"

During the summers here in Mount Hermon, I run the swim school. Most of the students are regulars who enjoy playing in the water as toddlers and begin swim instruction as preschoolers. Over the summers they learn to swim using proper form.

Some children who move into the community at age eight or older have never had swimming lessons. Although many of them have taught themselves to paddle around in the water, they haven't learned to swim correctly. The pool staff refers to this style of swimming as "jungle swimming."

"Oh wow! Wesley" was a classic example of a jungle swimmer. (You'll soon see how he got his nickname.) Wesley came to the pool for his first lesson at the age of ten. After a skills test which revealed he could swim only on his back, Wesley was placed in my class with four kindergarteners.

"Oh wow!" he complained. "I'm in a class of midgets! But I can swim! Can't I swim with my friends?"

I thought the situation over carefully. Tall, red-headed Wesley did look like a giant next to the little kids splashing around him. Even worse, his five year old sister was in the same class.

"Okay, Wes," I said sympathetically. "You can try to keep up with Matt's class over there. But if it doesn't work out, don't be upset if Matt sends you back."

"Oh wow!" Wesley breathed with obvious relief, "Thanks!"

"Listen up," Matt said, calling his group to attention. "Let's review your strokes, starting with breaststroke. Dive in, do one lap, and wait on the other side for the rest of the class to finish. Jordan, you go first."

Jordan dove in, and swam across. Wesley watched him intently. "Oh wow," he muttered worriedly to himself. "Oh wow!"

"Ready Wes? Do you know how to dive?" Matt asked, seeing his hesitation.

"Of course I can dive!" insisted the boy.

With that, he launched himself into the pool like a turtle hurled from a slingshot. Bystanders groaned as his body smacked loudly into the water. This was followed by an explosion of splashing.

"That kid looks like an underwater prize fighter!" exclaimed one of his classmates.

All of us watched in awe as Wesley attempted to swim the normally smooth breaststroke.

"He's not getting anywhere, Matt," I yelled. "Get him to roll over! He can swim on his back."

"Roll over, Wesley! Roll over!" The cry was taken up by his instructor and the spectators. To everyone's relief, Wesley rolled onto his back. With little fuss he made it to the opposite side.

"Oh wow!" Wesley gasped. "That's harder than it looks. Maybe I'll start with the other class. I don't wanna try that again!"

In spite of his greater age and strength, Wesley had difficulty keeping up with his beginner's class. He felt safe paddling on his back, and was reluctant to learn to swim properly. Fortunately, Wesley didn't give up. With great encouragement over the summers from his parents and the waterfront staff, he learned to let go of his fears and to relax in the water. This summer he reached his goal. He passed the Swimmers course and can now begin surfing with his father. The pool staff cheered his success with a rousing *"OH WOW!"*

Jungle Relators

Children who are not modelled and taught friendship skills become what I call *jungle relators*. They develop a form of social behavior which helps them to survive and even feel safe and in control. Unfortunately, these methods fail when it comes to developing quality friendships.

There is always hope for jungle relators, but progress can be slow and agonizing. Too often their fears become such obstacles that they cannot focus on learning the basic skills they need. Failure leads to discouragement and they become less willing to reach out to others.

Wesley's jungle swimming was due to the lack of early swimming lessons. Harley's jungle relating was due to neglect. Some children have problems learning friendship skills because they are taught by poorly trained parents or misguided friends.

"Just Do What I Do, Son"

"My Dad is a very successful salesman," Scott informed me. "He learned to get what he wanted from customers by using a big smile, a friendly greeting, and a great sales pitch. It worked so well on the job that he brought the same stuff home. After work he never had time to give my brother and me more than a forced smile, a hug and a "hello-how's-my-boys?" Conversations around the dinner table revolved around Dad telling Mom about the commissions he made that day using his ability to persuade. It was always the same.

"One day Dad gave me his big salesman's smile and said, 'It's good to see your getting interested in dating. But Mom tells me you're upset when a girl turns you down. Now son, making friends involves selling yourself a little. Always greet the girl by name and ask how she's doing. That's called charm. Get her interested in you by telling her something interesting about yourself or offering her something she wants. A big, handsome kid like you—she won't be able to resist!'

"Dad did his best and he succeeded on some levels," Scott continued. "Mom fell for it, didn't she? I tried Dad's method. It looks like it works. I know everyone at school by name. I was voted *Friendliest Senior* by my classmates last year. But that's as far as it goes. Beyond the *hello-how-are-you* stage, I have no real friends. Neither does Dad. He knows a lot of people, but they don't ask him over for dinner."

"Stick With Me, I'm Cool"

"Are you still playing the piano?" I asked Amy at our twentieth high school reunion. "You were the only one I knew who rushed home to practice because you enjoyed it!"

"I still play once in a while," the lovely woman next to me replied. "But the urgency's gone. Playing the piano was my release. High school was painful for me. Banging on the keys helped me let out my frustrations."

"That's surprising," I commented curiously. "You seemed happy. Looking back, what would you say the problem was?"

"Well," began Amy nervously. "Do you remember how close Kate and I always were? People used to call us *Kate and DupliKate.* She was a special friend since second grade.

"Kate became really *cool* in the sixth grade and hung around with the *in* crowd at school. I felt grateful to be included in that crowd even though they made it obvious I was only tolerated because of Kate. They were pretty cruel sometimes. To get a laugh from her friends, Kate even ridiculed things I said."

"How could you stand it?" I probed.

"I learned to take it," admitted Amy. "My parents encouraged me to make new friends, but I panicked at the thought of leaving Kate. I feared she'd reject me, and constantly felt put down and alone with her crowd. Other kids thought I was *in*, but I really felt *out*. So I ran home and played the piano."

"Are you and Kate still friends?" I asked.

"No. Going away for college was good for me. Making new friends helped me realize how unhealthy my dependence on Kate was. She's here, you know. She's the blonde in the toga-like thing over there. That's her third husband, Bill."

Keeping Our Children Out of the Jungle

Friendship is an integral expression of love. We begin training our children in friendship skills at birth. From the time they are babies, they develop attitudes about themselves. These attitudes continue over the span of their lives.

The Norse family adopted two toddlers from Korea. Danny had been nursed, cared for, and loved by his mother for eighteen months. Then she died and he was put up for adoption. Jenny was given to an orphanage at birth. She lay in a crib and was fed, changed, and touched only three times a day for over a year.

Once they arrived in America, Danny and Jenny were brought up as brother and sister in the same environment, with the same kind and amounts of attention, care, and discipline.

"We saw the difference their early care made from the first day we got them," their adoptive mother commented. "Danny was always a content, positive, caring boy who seemed to have inner reserves that enabled him to reach out to others. Jenny lacked those reserves. She tried to be as normal as her friends in everything she did, but underneath her public veneer was a volcano which smoked and burbled when she was asked to give of her time, energy, or emotions. She was difficult to live with because all her decisions were based on what *she* wanted and what was in her best interest."

Danny is now happily married and feels fulfilled in his life. Jenny is unhappily single. She travels the world, working awhile here and there, looking for the love she missed as a baby.

Babies need to be loved. They develop security and trust as we nourish, hold, burp, cuddle, rock, and interact with them. From the security of being loved, babies grow up able to love themselves, reach out and love others. This is the foundation for friendship.

As children grow older, the way we model friendship skills for them is critical. Talking and reading about friendship is not enough. If we talk the skills of friendship but fail to practice the skills within our families, our children will list us as phonies. ("Oh, I am *so* embarrassed!")

When you demonstrate friendship skills, remember that all four steps are necessary: explanation, demonstration, supervision, and practice.

When I joined the elementary school band in fourth grade I was one of fourteen beginning flute players. On Monday, the first day of class, our instructor misjudged his time and left himself only a few minutes to spend with the flute section. He gave us a short demonstration on how to hold our instruments, then handed out a fingering chart of the notes. We were sent home with instructions to learn a simple scale for the next class.

On Tuesday, when our turn came to show off what we learned, we held our flutes high and began blowing as hard as we could. Some of us started on high C, others an octave lower. At least half of us came out with notes that aren't even on the scale. As no one had explained the dangers of blowing too hard and hyperventilating, four students fainted. Bedlam followed as music stands and chairs crashed under the falling bodies.

Wednesday morning the apologetic teacher spent the entire hour teaching us how to *blow* properly into the mouthpiece of our instruments. Shaping his lips and then ours with his fingers, he drilled us in proper blowing techniques.

"Gently, gently, please blow oh so gently," I remember him chanting as he went from student to student.

This time no one fainted. By the end of the year we were playing recognizable tunes. I'm sure Mr. Brighton never again forgot the value of demonstration and supervision in his beginning band classes.

In eighth grade a boy I met at school asked me to go steady with him. After two dates, I realized I was uncomfortable feeling committed to him. I pondered over how to break up with Rick without hurting his feelings. Finally, I went to my mother for help.

"Tell Rick the positive things first," she coached. "You've enjoyed your outings with his family and have appreciated his great sense of humor and interest in you. He's a special guy, but you're just not ready to go steady. Emphasize *your* feelings as the problem, not his behavior. Tell him you'd like to be friends with him, and then be friendly and unembarrassed when you see him. Practice what you plan to say so you feel comfortable when you talk to him."

I did as Mom suggested. Rick and I went through junior high, high school, and college together. We remained friends. I cheered at his basketball games. He taught me to cross-country ski. Rick rejoiced when Randy and I got engaged, and he attended our wedding. What could have come to a painful end developed into a lasting friendship thanks to Mom's wise coaching and practice.

Once children sincerely want to make friends, they can master the skills needed to be a friend. Notice how that is put, because the thrust of what we'll discuss is that to make friends one must first become expert at being a friend.

Identifying Weaknesses in OUR *Friendship Skills*

It is often difficult to teach the skills of friendship by example in the home. We may be jungle relators ourselves. We may understand and practice some of the skills of friendship but fail with others. The problem is to identify the skills we are missing and to acknowledge personal weaknesses honestly. The solution is to accept that we, too, can change and actively work on skills that will bring us quality relationships.

Mastering friendship skills seems to come in layers. Just when I think I've learned to deal with a problem, providence presents me with the same problem at a deeper level. This brings the story of Eustace Clarence Scrubb to mind. His story is told in *The Voyage of the Dawn Treader* by C.S. Lewis. I've been known to emphasize certain points when reading it to my children.

Eustace is about ten. He is rude, snobbish, disrespectful, sneaky and unlikable. His ignorance about how to get along with others reminds me occasionally of my own children. The crew of the *Dawn Treader* can't stand him. Although they try to avoid him, Eustace goes out of his way to be unpleasant. The crew is torn between relief and terror when, on an enchanted island, Eustace turns into a dragon. He still has his human mind, but now is shackled with a heavy, scaled, ugly fire-breathing body.

Eustace can't stay on the ship. Talking and eating with the crew is unthinkable. Eustace finds that he is lonely—big time lonely. After awhile, Eustace realizes how nasty he has been. He wants to make amends. My children have trouble applying this part to themselves. They prefer to focus on the drama of life as a dragon.

"I kinda wouldn't mind being a dragon if I could fly," announces Jordan.

"Well, you'd have to find a new roommate cause I'm not sleeping with a stinky dragon!" responds Ben.

At one point Eustace is visited by Aslan, the great Lion. Aslan takes the dragon to a deep well, and commands him to undress and bathe in the water. Eustace tries to obey, but when he takes off the first layer of dragon scales he discovers another layer underneath. When he tries to take off that layer, he finds yet another layer. Aslan suggests that he be allowed to undress the boy. Desperately, Eustace agrees.

The pain of having his dragon skin torn off scale by scale is agonizing. But when Aslan finishes, his scaly skin stays off and, scratched and stinging, Eustace bathes in the well. As he washes, he discovers he's a boy again.

Aslan then dresses Eustace in new clothes. I try to work in a sentence or two of explanation for the children in case they've missed the point: "These clothes are kindness, goodness, respect. . . without which we all turn into dragons." They've taken to reading over my shoulder to make sure I stick to the printed words.

Eustace gratefully rejoins the crew. He apologizes for his former beastly behavior and, as Lewis notes, "the cure had begun."

Working on ourselves and with our children, Randy and I are trying to uncover the dragon scales and mislearned friendship habits that we're hauling around. We know they are there. Sometimes we see a whole dragon-full of scales, sometimes only one layer is revealed at a time. But as friendship is a process, we discover them when we dare to look. *The Friendship Self-Inventory* in the next chapter will help identify dragon scales so that they can be confronted and dealt with as our cure begins.

SUGGESTED ASSIGNMENT:

As you get underway, you may find it helpful to build a family ALL-STAR FRIENDSHIP BOOK. Using a notebook or binder, compile stories of outstanding or inspiring acts of friendship. Ask your children, parents, grandparents, friends and neighbors to relate friendship experiences that have blessed their lives. Write them down in your book. You'll find you have a treasury of encouragement as you work at teaching and learning friendship skills. As an added benefit, you will find that when you practice these listening and affirmation skills, a new closeness will develop between you and the storytellers.

The following example will give you ideas on how to set up your personal or family book.

The Beck Family ALL-STAR FRIENDSHIP BOOK.

Story from: Grandma Ruth Graham Allen

Told to: Keidi Beck

Today's date: 7-9-92

Date and Place
  of Story: 1961, Crescent Park Elementary School, Mr.
                  Niebauer's 5th Grade Class, Palo Alto, California.

When your Uncle Steven was in fifth grade, there was a boy in his class named Albert. Albert was small, uncoordinated, and far-sighted. He had big ears. His allergies kept him from closing his mouth when he breathed, and he wheezed and snorted most of the time. All of these problems conspired to make Albert the class scapegoat.

"Steven," his teacher reported to Grandma at a parent-teacher conference, "is the bravest boy I know. When his classmates harass and tease Albert, Steven moves next to him and stands quietly by his side. He refuses to be drawn into the teasing. He doesn't yell or say anything. But his standing by Albert helps diffuse the other children's enthusiasm for cruelty and they leave Albert alone."

Friendship Qualities Illustrated by the Story:

Kindness, loyalty, bravery.

If you don't know where you're going,
you'll probably end up somewhere else.
--L.J. Peter

The Friendship Self-Inventory

The goal of the *Friendship Self-Inventory* is to reveal the areas where our friendship skills need the most work. With this awareness, we can shed dragon scales and learn to relate to people in healthy ways.

The questions are grouped under headings that correspond to the chapters where the specific skills are discussed. If you find your weakest skills to be grouped in one area, you may choose to concentrate on the chapter(s) that cover the development of those skills. It may be helpful to refer back to the *Inventory* before beginning each chapter. This will help you focus on your personal needs as you set about mastering the skills of friendship.

When working on this inventory, pray for a hearing heart, think carefully, and answer honestly.

This inventory is not recommended for children under ten. To help those over that age to use it productively, follow a simple two-step process. First, have them read it carefully and complete it by themselves. Then lovingly review their work with them. Stress their strengths. Discuss gently with them one or two areas where they can build on those strengths to improve their less developed friendship skills. Use specific examples where possible. Remember, you are encouraging the children to wholeness, not humiliating or punishing them. If a child is resistant to having friendship skills examined in this way, drop the matter. Read the inventory aloud together. Then skip right on to Chapter 3 and begin learning the skills.

For a real eye-opener as to how friendship skills are being modelled in your home, complete this inventory with your spouse or with an older child. Each of you answer every statement for yourself and then as you perceive your spouse or child will (or should) answer the statement. Review the conclusions gently and honestly together.

As parents, you will want to be mutually encouraging without humiliating or punishing each other. It hurts to be criticized. If you feel criticism is needed, try to accompany it with large doses of affirmation. Here's the technique: whenever you can do so truthfully, say a positive word before a critical word. For example: "Son, you are great at greeting people when they come to the house. Both Grandpa and Mrs. Jones commented on it today. Your friendship skills will improve even more as you practice talking about your friends and their interests and not about yourself. All of us have been impressed by how hard you are working on these skills."

For privacy, answer the questions in pencil or on a separate piece of paper.

Check those answers that apply to you.

FRIENDLINESS (Chapter 4)

AS A FRIEND, I TEND TO:

1. _____ *rarely invite others to my home.*

   _____ enjoy inviting others over.

2. _____ *be lonely and feel friendless or deserted.*

_____ reach out to others when I'm feeling lonely.

3. _____ *be too shy to introduce myself to people.*

_____ be known for my friendliness.

4. _____ *avoid greeting people I don't know very well.*

_____ go out of my way to introduce myself to strangers.

LISTENING (Chapter 5)

AS A FRIEND I TEND TO:

5. _____ *be so anxious to talk that I don't really hear.*

_____ listen carefully to what friends say.

6. _____ *talk a lot.*

_____ try not to talk more than I listen.

7. _____ *be judgmental, rather than understanding.*

_____ pursue my friends' thoughts to ensure I understand them.

8. _____ *turn conversations back to myself.*

_____ encourage friends to talk about themselves.

9. _____ *get annoyed when people talk to me during a television program or when I'm reading.*

_____ be willing to listen most of the time.

10. _____ *use "I" in almost every sentence I speak.*

_____ make sure a friend has finished talking about a subject before bringing up my own interests.

GIVING (Chapters 6 and 7)

AS A FRIEND I TEND TO:

11. _____ *cringe inwardly when asked to serve others.*

_____ be willing to help where and when I can.

12. _____ *complain a lot.*

_____ discuss problems calmly and noncritically.

13. _____ *rarely volunteer to help solve the problems I complain about.*

_____ look for solutions to problems before discussing them.

14. _____ *have a hard time saying "thank you."*

_____ be good about saying "thank you."

15. _____ *not like to compliment others.*

_____ enjoy telling people how well they are doing.

16. _____ *have trouble acknowledging friends' successes and growth.*

_____ rejoice with friends as they grow.

17. _____ *feel like I'm always rushing to meet the urgent needs of friends.*

_____ set realistic boundaries as to where I can and cannot help friends get their needs met.

18. _____ *be shy about expressing love to friends.*

_____ be sincere and bold about expressing love to friends.

19. _____ *have trouble asking for help.*

_____ ask friends for help when I really need it.

COURTESY (Chapter 8)

AS A FRIEND I TEND TO:

20. _____ *be late a lot.*

_____ try to make a point of being on time.

21. _____ *rarely return borrowed items on time or in good shape.*

_____ be prompt in returning borrowed items and make a point of seeing that they are in good shape.

22. _____ *say I'll do something and then fail to carry through on my commitment.*

_____ not commit myself to something unless I'm sure I can really do it.

23. _____ *cry, sulk, or pout when friends (mother, father, spouse) don't do things my way.*

_____ accept the things I cannot change and try to maintain a good attitude.

24. _____ *give my friends the "icy silence" treatment when I'm mad at them.*

_____ talk over difficulties with my friends.

25. _____ *want one close friend I can spend most of my time with.*

_____ try to develop several meaningful friendships.

26. _____ *be jealous when a friend tells me how much he enjoys being with someone else.*

_____ recognize and appreciate my friends' other friendships.

TRAINING THE TONGUE (Chapter 9)

AS A FRIEND I TEND TO:

27. _____ *make untrue excuses when I have failed a friend.*

_____ apologize when I have failed a friend.

28. _____ *gossip about others with friends.*

_____ keep my friends' confidences.

29. _____ *interrupt when a friend is telling a story or joke to correct the details.*

_____ quietly enjoy a friend's stories and jokes even when I know the details are incorrect.

30. _____ *avoid conflict at all costs.*

_____ speak up when I see a problem in our relationship.

31. _____ *hold grudges.*

_____ willingly forgive friends.

32. _____ *avoid contact with someone I've offended or who has offended me.*

_____ seek to heal wounds in friendships.

33. _____ *have hard time admitting it when I'm wrong.*

_____ freely admit it and apologize when I'm wrong.

34. _____ *be quick to anger and slow to forgive.*

_____ be slow to anger and quick to forgive.

FAIRNESS IN OUR EXPECTATIONS (Chapter 10)

AS A FRIEND I TEND TO:

35. _____ *feel like people should be doing things for me.*

_____ look for ways to be helpful.

36. _____ *be demanding about getting what I want.*

_____ be good at sharing.

37. ____ *compare myself negatively or positively to others.*

____ admire people without having to be like them.

38. ____ *be disappointed when friends do not give me the praise or recognition I think I deserve.*

____ try to focus on people's strengths instead of their weaknesses.

LOYALTY (Chapter 11)

AS A FRIEND I TEND TO:

39. ____ *abandon a friendship when the going gets tough.*

____ stand by friends through misunderstandings.

40. ____ *back away from friends who are being attacked or are in trouble.*

____ be loyal to friends.

41. ____ *stick with friendships that are unhealthy for me.*

____ recognize when people are using or abusing my friendship.

ENCOURAGING EACH OTHER TO WHOLENESS (Chapter 12)

AS A FRIEND I TEND TO:

42. ____ *use sarcasm in my humor.*

____ try not to tease friends in any hurtful way.

43. ____ *swear at friends when I get angry at them.*

____ blow off steam without embittering others.

44. ____ *cover for my friends' problems when they get themselves into trouble.*

____ allow friends to live with the consequences of their own mistakes.

45. ____ *do nothing to stop friends when they are heading for trouble.*

____ caution friends if I think they are on the wrong track.

46. ____ *join in wrongdoing with friends to prove my loyalty to the relationship.*

____ refuse to join in wrongdoing with friends.

INTIMACY (Chapter 13 and 14)

AS A FRIEND I TEND TO:

47. _____ *keep my guard up so friends will see only the side of me I think they want to see.*

_____ allow myself to be real—happy, sad, grumpy, quiet, tired—with close friends.

48. _____ *make decisions based on what I think friends want me to do.*

_____ feel free to express my feelings honestly and make my own decisions.

49. _____ *have trouble acknowledging and sharing my feelings.*

_____ stay in touch with and accept my feelings as valid.

50. _____ *be reluctant to admit struggles and weaknesses.*

_____ share problems with close friends.

BAD HABITS I INDULGE IN THAT ARE STUMBLING BLOCKS TO FRIENDSHIP:
(such as a negative outlook, swearing, lying, bragging, not listening, etc.)

_____

_____

_____

_____

_____

_____

_____

MY STRONGEST FRIENDSHIP SKILLS ARE:

_____

_____

_____

_____

_____

MY WEAKEST FRIENDSHIP SKILLS ARE:

_____

_____

_____

_____

_____

There was a young woman from Bend,
Who could not seem to find a good friend;
When seen on the street
Not a person she'd greet
So she lived all alone 'til her end.

Casual Friendships:
Meetings and Greetings

Eight months after Harley joined our family he asked to join a children's club he'd heard about at school. I called the club leader and explained Harley's interest.

"You called just in time," Mrs. Doyal replied. "We're just starting our new group and there's still space. We also need help rather desperately. Are you available?"

I volunteered to teach Native American crafts and games during the October meetings and to organize the holiday project. Mrs. Doyal asked me to bring lasagne for twenty people to the introductory potluck the following weekend.

The night of the dinner arrived. Harley was beside himself with excitement. Dressed in his best, he eagerly helped load the casserole, the diaper bag, and our two toddlers into the car. We arrived at the hall and signed in. No one greeted us. Randy set the casserole on the food table.

"Is Mrs. Doyal here?" I asked the man working on the sound system.

He pointed to a tiny woman sitting nearby. I introduced my family to her.

"I'm glad you came," she told us. "Why don't you sit over there," she added, pointing to an end table. "Dinner is about to start."

An enormous man wearing a red stocking cap stood up at the microphone.

"I am *The Tapper*," he told us. "When I tap your table, it is your turn to get food from the serving table. Try to keep your children at your table rather than letting them run around. And remember," he added, shaking a finger at the crowd teasingly, *"don't head for the food line until I've tapped you!"*

For half an hour we watched this giant elf tap all of the other tables. Harley was too wound up to sit still. Randy gave him a crash course on introductions, took him by the hand and let him introduce himself to the neighboring tables.

"Hi," I heard Harley recite, "I'm Harley Thompson. This is my Dad-for-now, Randy Beck. What are your names?"

People acknowledged Randy and Harley, but no one encouraged conversation. Harley asked all the questions. He was answered without enthusiasm. The man in the red hat detoured over to Randy and Harley and suggested they sit down and wait to be tapped.

Other people finished eating and began visiting. Their banter suggested they knew each other well. No one spoke to us. The elf served his dinner and sat down. Exasperated, Randy told the man in the red hat that we hadn't been tapped yet.

"Oh yeah," he replied. "Go ahead."

We grabbed our plates and headed for the table. Harley got there first. His wail pierced the air.

"There's nothing left! They ate all our dinner! I'm hungry!"

Harley was right. Except for a few crumbs left on the dessert table, every pan was scraped clean. At the sound of Harley's cries, people turned towards us. A few stared briefly, then turned back to their heaping plates. No one acknowledged our plight or offered help.

"They probably hope that if they ignore the problem it will go away," Randy whispered to me. "The children have hit melt down and you're near tears. Let's go."

We collected our empty casserole dish and walked out. With us went the craft classes and the holiday project. I called Mrs. Doyal and told her that Harley and I were unable to deal with such unfriendliness. She apologized and admitted "perhaps the group had become a bit exclusive." We never heard from her again.

Friendliness

Friendship begins with friendliness. When we greet people with a cheerful *hello*, introduce ourselves, and express interest in who they are, we welcome them into our world. Everyone wants to feel needed and important. That's the basis for self-esteem and wholeness. Our greeting says "You are important to me—I want to know you." That makes people feel good about themselves. People who help other people feel good never lack friends.

When Imke Keissling came from Germany to work at Mount Hermon, she stretched her legs after the long flight by taking a walk.

"People here are so friendly," she told us on her return. "They greet me, a stranger. They smile. Some say more than *hello*. When they find I am a foreigner they ask many questions. They want to know my name. I am not sure—is it safe? I am surprised but it makes me feel very good."

I grew up in an era and neighborhood where social graces were something our parents *hoped* we'd grow up to need and use. To encourage us in this direction, in the sixth grade boys and girls were sent to Bedoin's School of Ballroom Dance.

Mrs. Bedoin looked like Ginger Rogers with Tammi Baker make-up. Her husband wore the thin black moustache of an aging Zorro. And although we thought they were dinosaurs, the Bedoins taught us manners.

"When you introduce yourself, do it with a smile. Look right into your new friend's eyes. Use your first and last name," I remember

Mrs. Bedoin telling us. "When you introduce one friend to another, always present the older person first if one is obviously older. 'Mr. Tom Smith, I'd like you to meet my friend, Miss Sarah Jones.' Seal the greeting with a firm handshake and a reply such as 'I'm pleased to meet you, Mr. Smith.' Now boys, turn to your partner and practice this."

Embarrassing? You bet. Worthwhile? Then, we thought not. Now, absolutely yes.

Friendliness Begins at Home

In our home, we are teaching the children, including preschoolers, to greet and acknowledge every visitor. Nathan enjoys this. Distant relatives, strangers, repair men, wrong numbers, all receive Nathan's warm greeting and interest.

It was harder for Laurel. When she was four, she'd bury her face in my lap when asked to greet a visitor. Attempts to persuade her to say a simple hello were fruitless. Laurel felt uncomfortable when attention was focused on her. She would break away and run off to play with her friends. To help her learn, we asked her to stay and greet the guests. She could then excuse herself if she so wished. Laurel hid her head in my lap the first few times, but soon her shy smile appeared and she quietly welcomed our company. We congratulated her and thanked her for her courage and politeness. Now, at seven, Laurel is known for her cheerful greetings. A tiny battle was won.

What Comes After The Greeting

Our family has learned some simple steps that help both adults and children get closer to people they meet. The first step is simply *saying hello*. Second, is to *observe the reaction* of a potential new friend. Does she return a friendly overture or does she ignore us or respond unenthusiastically? Step three depends on the signals we've received. Here we decide whether *to pursue the friendship further,* or *to stop and back away.* Assuming we've received welcoming signals, we begin investing more time and energy in the new friendship.

As a freshman in college, I lived in Germany. Many of the students were from military families stationed overseas. We were all far from home. Our dorm mother informed me of the extreme homesickness of two students, Susanna and Katrina. She asked me, as the residence assistant, to introduce them to others and make them feel welcome.

Susanna was easy. She responded with delight to my greeting. We exchanged basic information about ourselves. "I am from Naarden, Holland," she told me. "This is my first time away from my family. I've been crying a lot. And how about you? Where is your family?" she added with a smile.

"They're in California, near San Francisco," I said.

"Oh," Susanna responded cheerfully, "perhaps you know my cousin, Carolyn Leigh? She lives in Los Angeles."

I chuckled and asked, "Perhaps you know my neighbor, Claes Wyckoff? He moved to Amsterdam!"

We both laughed.

"Would you like to go for a walk before dinner?" I asked.

"Oh yes," Susanna replied enthusiastically.

That was the beginning of a special friendship. Susanna and I found we had many interests and experiences in common as we hiked the forests and farmlands around the college. Friendships came easily to Susanna. Her interest in others eased her homesickness and she eagerly entered into college life.

Some people don't respond well to such a direct approach. The signals I received from Katrina taught me what to look for when someone doesn't want to be pursued.

"Hello, Katrina! I'm Terry, the resident assistant here in the Schloss," I said cheerfully, referring to the castle in which the college housed women students.

"Hello." Katrina gave her reply to the floor, where she focused her gaze.

"Have you found your way around Katrina? Can I help you get settled?" I asked.

"I'm fine." Katrina replied, still looking down.

Realizing that yes or no questions would not open up the conversation, I asked Katrina where she was from.

"Pakistan." she volunteered without enthusiasm.

"Pakistan!" I exclaimed. "You look like the model on a 'Welcome to Sweden' travel poster. How did your family end up in Pakistan?"

"My Dad's job." she contributed.

"Wow," I hedged, searching for a question that would spark her interest. "What do you like best about Pakistan?"

"Not being there," Katrina stated as she turned on her heel and walked away.

I got the hint. Katrina was homesick but not for Pakistan. She didn't want to talk about herself. At the next opportunity I tried a different tactic.

"Hello Katrina! How are things going?" I asked.

"Okay." she replied.

"We are trying to get some student activities organized, Katrina. Would you be interested in music, drama, travel, sports, or anything like that?" I asked.

"No," she commented. "I like to read during my spare time."

I plunged to the heart of the matter. "Don't you get lonely, Katrina? Mrs. Burke told me you were homesick. The school activities are fun. We're going to help pick grapes this weekend and then join in the town harvest celebration. It's a good way to meet people. We even get paid for picking. Do you want to join us?"

"I don't think so," she replied. "But have fun. And Terry," she added, "don't worry about me. If I want friends, I'll find them, okay?"

Les Giblin, in his booklet *Skill With People* suggests bluntly: "When you are talking to people, pick out the most interesting subject in the world to them to talk about. What is the most interesting subject in the world to them? THEMSELVES! When you talk to them about themselves they will be deeply interested and utterly fascinated. They will think well of you for doing this."

I thought long and hard about this quote. People enjoy talking about themselves. We can show genuine interest in new acquaintances by asking them questions about who they are and what they enjoy. This is a great way to get to know them. But there must be a balance, a give and take in the conversation. Only if there is mutual warmth and interest do we find ourselves wanting to learn more about a new friend. Listening to people talk about themselves all the time can leave us bored to tears.

The last step, therefore involves *sharing oneself*. This is vital because if new friends do not want to learn about our lives or if we do not offer to open our thoughts and feelings to them, the friendship will be limited in its health and growth.

Hospitality

One of the best ways to begin investing in a new friend is to extend hospitality. Share lunch (sharing food is symbolic of hospitality and acceptance) or invite a new friend to your home. Parents play a key role here. I continually ask myself, "Is my home welcoming to my children's friends? Is my heart? Do I encourage my children to be hospitable by inviting their friends and the families of their friends into our home?" I've learned that the occasion doesn't have to be fancy or expensive. Popcorn and games. A hike and a picnic. Ice cream. An overnight. When our house was small, we invited people to the park for outings.

I struggle with wanting our home to be a sanctuary for our children and their friends and yet dreading the extra noise, the litter, the grocery bills. But what are the alternatives? Randy and I like having our children hang out under our wings. Knowing where they are and that they are safe is crucial to our job as parents. We work on ways to model hospitality and encourage our children to welcome their friends into our home and activities. And on rainy Saturdays when every cushion, blanket and pillow in the house turns the living room into a giant fort, I work on ways to remain sane.

Dealing With Unfriendliness

Randy was invited to a neighbor's home recently. He entered the house and greeted by name each of the three children who were sitting in the living room watching television. Not one of the children, aged 19, 16 and 12, glanced up to return his greeting.

"I felt like an invisible man," Randy chuckled.

Why is it that some people make a practice of avoiding casual contacts with others? Many children and some adults who act unfriendly are really shy. For other people, avoidance may come from a fear of rejection. For teenagers it often stems from fear of embarrassment.

We are trying to teach our children that it is not acceptable to deliberately avoid people we have met and know are safe. This approach hit a snag when Laurel, who was five at the time, met Joe, a big, very tall man who visits us occasionally. Joe loves children. He greeted Laurel by snatching her offered hand, lifting her into the air and swinging her merrily around and around. Laurel felt invaded. The next time Joe came she refused to leave her room. When her Dad asked her about this she explained her fears to him.

"If you are uncomfortable with Joe, or with anyone, Laurel, you do not have to shake hands with them." Randy told her. "In this case, I'll hold your hand and you can just say hello, okay? I know that Joe is a safe person. He didn't mean to scare you. But, we can talk to him about your concerns and let him know how you feel. When someone really scares you, hon, always trust your own feelings and run to us for help."

Breaking down Unfriendliness Barriers

Unfriendliness may be so deliberate that breaking down its walls requires tact, persistence, and sometimes, courage.

When Keidi made the seventh grade volley-ball team, she discovered that some of the other girls on the team were part of a cool crowd who resented her uncool presence. For most of the season, they snubbed her. Keidi often came home from practice in tears. She wanted to quit. We discussed the problem with her and suggested she pray for a positive attitude and adopt a strategy of *unfailing friendliness*. This involved being friendly towards her teammates and encouraging them whenever she could.

"I understand what you're saying," she told us. "Friendly and encouraging I can do. Pretending to be part of their crowd or that I don't mind the way they treat me I can't do. But I'll try to detach from the mean stuff and be myself."

By the end of the season, Keidi was enjoying volleyball and making friends on the team. She received the trophy for being the *Most Inspirational Player* at the final awards assembly. Four years later volleyball is a major activity for Keidi. She and her varsity teammates have matured into a cohesive unit and enjoy travelling and competing together.

Remember. . .

Casual friendships stem from our informal contact with people we see and interact with in daily life, but with whom we don't spend significant time. These are classmates, teachers, and neighbors. These casual interactions may be superficial but they are critical because they can open doors for deeper friendships.

Casual friendships begin with friendliness. Welcome newcomers with a smile, a kind word, and an introduction. Cheerfully greet people by name when possible. Show genuine interest in others by asking them questions about themselves and their activities. Reach out, observe, pursue, and find space to share yourself.

The stage is set. We're practicing friendliness. Our new

acquaintance has been welcomed and hospitality has been extended. Now we are ready to learn the skills that will support more meaningful friendships.

DISCUSSION QUESTIONS:

1) Think of two of the friendliest people you know.

2) Name three things about their friendliness that impress you.
   1.
   2.
   3.

3) How do you feel after you have been cheerfully greeted by a casual friend?

4) What qualities attract you to a person when you are seeking to begin a new friendship?

5) Think of three questions you can ask casual acquaintances to show your interest in them.
   1.
   2.
   3.

6) Describe a situation in your life where *unfailing friendliness* could have or did help you overcome feelings of isolation or rejection.

ASSIGNMENT: Introduce yourself to someone new or someone who's been around but whom you really don't know. Remember the person's name. Find out three interesting facts about this person. Discuss the facts you learned with your parents. Evaluate how the introduction went and how you felt about it. Was it as difficult as you thought it would be? What was your new friend's reaction? Plan a strategy for a follow-up conversation.

listen \ `lis- n\ verb
to hear with thoughtful attention; to focus
or concentrate on a conversation,
speech, or sound.

Meaningful Friendships Begin with Listening Skills

The school was Stanford. The class was Sociology. The first part of the assignment was to tape record our major conversations for two days. When class met again, we talked for a few minutes before the professor appeared. Many of us were confident that we'd captured some brilliant ideas on our tapes and were modestly willing to share them with the class.

But the professor's assignment surprised us all. We were to transcribe our tapes and tally how many times we used the word *I*, interrupted, or changed the focus of the conversation from one subject back to ourselves. Had we verbally expressed our understanding of what the person we were talking to was saying?

Listening to myself talk on the tape recorder for two days was enlightening. When our class met the following week, we worked as a group to evaluate the combined statistics of our listening skills and write guidelines that would help us become good listeners.

We came up with three categories of good listening. They were *focused listening, listening to understand, and not self-centering the conversation.* Our professor looked at our report and remarked, "In the seven years I've been doing this exercise, the conclusions of the students have always been very similar. You've discovered that you, like everyone else, like to talk about yourselves. As sociologists, you must learn to be genuinely interested in other people. You express this interest when you find out what interests someone else and listen to them talk about it. Then and only then," he concluded, "do you earn the right to offer your point of view."

Focused Listening

Learning to focus on people and what they are trying to tell us is a skill. It takes concentration and practice. Failure to learn can wound us in our closest relationships.

Ned came home from school. He'd just been selected to represent his school at the state bicentennial celebration. He was bursting with the good news. Unfortunately, he entered the house during the final scenes of Mom's afternoon soap opera.

"Can I talk to you, Mom?" he asked hesitantly.

"Sure, go ahead!" replied Mom, not taking her eyes from the screen.

"It's really important," said Ned.

"I've just got to know if Darrell's lover really murdered his long-lost sister. But go ahead, honey. I'm listening," Mom insisted, still not making eye contact with the eager child.

"Never mind." sighed Ned. As he left the house he heard the rising music signalling the end of Mom's program. But he was discouraged. Mom was unwilling to give him the full, focused attention he would have appreciated. The keen edge of his excitement was been dulled. He did not care to try again.

Kent had been upset all morning at school. His dog, Tasha, had escaped from the yard during the night and had not returned home by the time Kent left the house. Kent was cheered when Brittani sat next to him at recess.

"What's up, Kent? You look sad." Brittani commented.

"Thanks for asking," Kent replied. "I've had an awful morning."

Kent began to pour out Tasha's story. As he told Brittani about the family search party he noticed that she was busy looking for friends in the recess crowd. She interrupted often to wave or call out a *hello*. When Kent saw she was focused elsewhere, he gave a big sigh. He wrapped up his story and moved away.

Realizing what she'd done, Brittani ran after Kent. She apologized for letting herself get distracted. She told Kent she really wanted to hear about Tasha and asked him to try again.

Kent was surprised, but he thanked Brittani and said he was glad she cared about his problems. This time she gave Kent her full attention. She looked directly at him and listened with her eyes. She could tell from his expression and body language that he was really upset. Kent told her that Tasha was due to have her first litter of puppies any time. Brittani suggested getting together a search party at lunch break.

Kent was really pleased and they did find Tasha. She'd crawled into a big packing box near their garage to have the puppies. All the kids and one of the teachers came to watch the birth. Kent thanked Brittani again for her help. They agreed it had been one of the best afternoons of their lives.

Listening to Understand

We sometimes forget that understanding takes more than the simple act of listening.

Claire arrived at her junior high school one morning looking bedraggled.

"Claire, what's wrong?" asked her friend Mattie sympathetically.

"Something caught fire in the garage last night. My room, the kitchen, and the garage burned down completely before the firemen could control the flames. We are all fine, but everything I owned, except what was in the laundry, was destroyed." related Claire sadly.

"Oh my gosh, that's terrible! Did you hear that Mark and Sam? Claire's room burned down last night! You poor thing! Why, that's just so awful," Mattie gushed loudly. "No wonder you look kind of down. That's about the worst thing that could happen! I know exactly how you feel, Claire. We've never had a fire, but I understand how bad you must feel. Really, I do!"

Claire looked at her friend and shook her head. She knew Mattie wasn't really trying to understand how she felt. After getting the bare facts from Claire, Mattie had launched into her dramatic response. She gushed. She exclaimed. She said she understood exactly how Claire felt, although she never lost her belongings in a fire. Mattie called on Mark and Sam to witness her expression of sympathy. She had something attention-getting to say, and she wanted others to notice immediately. Mattie turned Claire's misfortune into a way to grab some limelight for herself. Claire felt abandoned.

Here's another kind of response, one that reflects *listening to understand.*

"Oh Claire, what a blow!" exclaimed Mattie, giving her friend a hug. "Were you scared?"

"I was terrified. Even after I knew that we were all safe, I kept feeling like part of me was dying in the flames. It's still unbelievable!"

"I can tell you're really shaken up, Claire." said Mattie. "Can I help clean up the mess or go shopping for new clothes with you? Coming to school today was very brave. I've gotta go, but can we meet at recess and talk some more?"

This time, Mattie listened to understand Claire. She put compassion into action by listening. Claire's emotions were addressed. Mattie said she was brave! That encouragement helped Claire get through the turmoil of the next few days.

Most of us have, over the years, learned to listen only for the purpose of giving a response. In school, my tendency was to listen carefully to the teachers until I knew what answer they wanted. Then I stopped listening, raised my hand, and concentrated on being heard.

When *listening to understand,* I've learned to listen to my friend's words, mood, and meaning without always thinking of a reply *while my friend is still talking.* This is a constant struggle. I've noticed how anxious I become to put in my two-cents worth and how, when focusing on making a response I stop listening. Eloise Mousalam has taught me some positive steps for improving listening skills.

Eloise runs a very successful beauty salon. Her customers are unusually loyal. Some have been with her since her beauty school days. One reason is that Eloise is an expert listener.

"How did you learn to be such a great listener?" I asked Eloise as she cut my hair one afternoon.

"Beauty salons and barber shops deal very closely with people," she told me. "If the customer is uneasy, no matter how good the cut is, they won't come back. Most of my customers love to talk. Few of them, especially the single ones, have someone who listens to them. I offer a sympathetic ear as a bonus to a good hairstyling. It's an unbeatable combination."

"Do you use any listening strategies when you have a customer in the chair?" I probed.

"I do," Eloise answered. "For one, I've found it's very important to remember names. Everyone likes that. Secondly, with new customers I try to find out about them—their jobs, their families, their hobbies. Once they've given me an idea of who they are, I make a point of remembering some of the details. That way, when they come in again I can ask how their bowling tournament went or if they're still walking every morning on the beach. I never give advice unless someone asks for it. I also ask people *feeling questions* like 'How did you feel about that?' or 'Weren't you scared?'

"Sometimes I really don't understand what these people are going through. Their experience is either totally outside of mine or is, in my book, a silly thing to be worked up about. In those cases I usually say, "I'm sorry you have to go through that. That must be really tough."

"Do customers ever try to find out who you are?" I asked.

"Some do," Eloise replied with a smile. "And those are the people I really enjoy. Some people don't really see me as a person. The ones who do are treasures. Every customer who walks in here gets my listening ear. The ones who also are concerned about me become more than customers—they become friends."

Remodeling the Self-Centered Conversation

Self-centering a conversation is a bit like offering a tantalizing pastry to someone, wafting it under their nose, and then grabbing it back and eating it. It has been my experience that many people who complain about not having friends indulge heavily in this habit. This practice is commonplace among children, and, sadly, many never outgrow it.

A child might say, "I can't get along with my teacher. He picks on me whenever I'm not prepared." Another child will jump in and say,

"Well, my teacher even asks questions about things that aren't in the assignment." The second child is trying one-upmanship to get the conversation back to himself, without showing any compassion or interest in the problem the first child expressed.

When Nathan was eight, he came in from the yard to show me a bleeding cut he had on his arm. Little brother Jordan looked at the wound for a minute, and then hauled up his pant leg to show me a scab he'd gotten several days earlier. Littler sister Laurel then got into the act by talking about an *owie* she'd had months ago.

I don't always catch these things, but this time I sat them all down and said, "We need to learn to listen and sympathize with someone without always bringing the conversation back to ourselves. Nathan has expressed concern about his cut. Let's give him some sympathy before we go into the details of past owies."

Jordan and Laurel put on dramatically sad faces and turned solemnly towards Nathan. "I'm sorry you hurt yourself, Nathan." Jordan said. Laurel puckered her lips and offered to kiss Nathan's cut. We all laughed. Nathan felt we'd offered proper attention to his cut, and all of the children had a brief lesson on listening.

We all bring the conversation back to ourselves at times. When we converse with friends, we need to talk about our own thoughts and experiences. If we don't reveal ourselves to friends, how can they know us? It becomes a problem only when we ignore the needs of others and make ourselves the primary topic.

The remedy for this was made clear in my sociology class. *Listening to myself talk* helped me notice how many times I interrupted or changed the conversation to bring it back to myself. I wince when faced with how many times *I* cropped up in my comments! My focus was usually on my story, my ideas, my opinions.

Remodeling weak conversational habits is a challenge. Being aware of the problems is the first step. Practicing new skills is the next.

When Jordan was eight, he went up to the snow with friends and learned to ski. He came home bubbling with the high adventure of it all. As Jordan described his escapades on the slopes, his older siblings were asked to think twice about how to identify with his adventure without talking about their own skiing experiences. In a family of eager talkers, there were long silences while the older ones thought out their responses.

I expected to hear one of them launch into "You thought the snow was icy? When I went last year..."

Instead, I heard Keidi saying, "Icy snow is the pits, isn't it, Jordan? Did you find it easy to fall and then hard to get up?"

Obviously, Keidi had skied in icy snow before. But Jordan was still the center of the conversation. The word *I* was not used.

Big brother Nathan asked, "Did you find that the inside of your legs got sore from snowplowing, Jordan?"

This question told Jordan that Nathan understood the strain of snowplowing, and yet Nathan invited his brother to express his experience without intruding his own.

Jordan's response to these questions was, "Yes, did that happen to you, too?" That opened the door for the others to retell their stories. Which they did with a sigh of relief, many *I* statements, and considerable gusto.

Remember. . .

Become aware of your listening skills by listening to yourself talk. Try to take some of the *I* out of your conversations. Think before responding. Be patient with yourself and with those around you who have not yet learned to put these skills into action. There must be time to share yourself if a friendship is going to work—but don't steal the time when a friend needs you to be a good listener.

DISCUSSION QUESTIONS:

Read the following responses. Decide which listening skills the respondent is not using *(focused listening, listening to understand,* and/or *self-centering the conversation).*

Discuss alternative responses that would demonstrate the healthy use of these skills.

1. "You made the team, Joe? I am sooo jealous!"

2. "I hope your graduation party was as fun as mine was! We had such a blast!"

3. "You had to be treated for lice, Cara? Move back, everyone! Cara has lice and I don't want to catch them from her!"

4. "You were homesick when you visited your Uncle John in Europe? Are you crazy? Most of us will never have the fun of traveling in Europe, and you got homesick?

5. "Hi Bobby! You don't look too good. You fell off your bike and now this shoulder hurts bad? You can't lift that arm? I've got baseball practice. See you later. Oh, don't forget to turn on the oven at five o'clock like Mom said. Okay?"

6. "You're quitting the track team, Carl? How come? You are so good at the field events. Burn-out is no excuse for someone with the kind of potential you have!"

7. "Ed picked you for his debate partner, Sally? Well, have I got news for you! Travis told me Bill wants to ask me out!"

ASSIGNMENT:

Listen to yourself talk during a family meal, a social occasion, and one-on-one with a friend. Be aware of how often you use the word *I* or talk about yourself.

*The person all wrapped up in himself
is a mighty small package.*

It is in giving that we receive.
--St. Francis of Assisi

Giving and Receiving—
Finding the Balance

Kaiser Cement Company owned a quarry on the other side of our mountain. Their motto, painted on the side of their bright pink cement trucks, was: "FIND A NEED AND FILL IT." This is the basic rule of giving. Kaiser succeeded in selling its cement because it found customers' needs and filled them with quality, service, and fair prices. As a company, it was a giver. Some of its competitors who were only interested in making a profit were takers. They did not do as well or failed outright.

We can learn to become givers. Just as love is action, not merely a feeling, so giving requires us to act—to do things for people by sharing who we are, what we have, and what we do. A giver is one *who is in the habit of giving.*

Look around. Does someone need a helping hand? Encouragement? Appreciation? A shoulder to cry on? This is an opportunity to take action and to master the skills of giving.

When Harley lived with us, an elderly neighbor was widowed and then suffered a heart attack. After she recovered, she continued to live on her own. One day Harley looked down from our deck and watched Bertie unload groceries from her car. Because of weakness, she unloaded and carried in one item at a time.

"Terry, wait'll you see this!" he yelled. "That old lady has the strangest way of carrying in groceries that you ever saw. At this rate she'll be another two hours getting the other two bags in."

"Mrs. Franklin has been very sick," I explained. "She's too weak to carry a whole bag of groceries. If you were sick and weak, wouldn't you like to have a healthy, strong neighbor boy come and help you unload your groceries?" I asked.

"Yeah, I sure would," Harley replied.

I stared at him for at least ten seconds. Harley didn't move a muscle.

"Do you think I could be that strong neighbor kid?" he asked finally.

"Yes!" I shouted with a sigh of relief. "Go for it, Harley!"

In a flash he was down the hill offering his services. It was Harley's first step in learning to find a need and fill it. Bertie (who Harley referred to as "my old lady") called and made appointments with Harley to unload groceries for her every time she shopped. Harley was rewarded with a satisfying new feeling—that of being needed.

There are many times when we find a need but don't want to help fill it. We're too busy. Too tired. It's boring. That person is difficult. There's no glamour or reward involved. Rewards, by the way, can take unexpected forms. Only by giving can we discover the blessing of helping others. Rewards come as bonuses rather than expectations.

Weldon Hardenbrook grew up during the '40s and '50s in San Jose when it was a small town surrounded by farms. The day the circus came to town, Weldon got up before dawn and rode his bike five miles out of town to watch the circus set up for the afternoon performance. Watching was the closest he'd get to seeing the circus, as his family was poor and Weldon couldn't afford a ticket. The lad biked around the train cars, stopping now and then to lean on the handlebars and absorb the sights and sounds around him. On one of these stops, an older man with a dog on a leash stood near Weldon.

"Young man," this gentleman said, "Would you be so kind as to hold my dog for me for awhile?"

Weldon gazed at the man thoughtfully. He'd planned to keep moving as the boxcar doors were opened down the line. He didn't want to be stuck in one place with a stranger's dog. But the man needed help and Weldon's father had taught him to be helpful, especially to the elderly.

"Yes, sir," he replied with a sigh.

"I'm not offering to pay you," the man said. "But I'll be mighty grateful."

Weldon got off of his bike and took the pup's leash as the man walked off. Although exciting things were happening just out of sight, Weldon stuck to his post faithfully until the dog's master returned.

"Son," the man addressed him with a smile, "you've done a great job. You helped me when I needed help. Now, if you'll stick with me I can get us into the restricted area and you can watch the elephants pull the tents up."

From that point on, Weldon's day took on a dream-like quality. Not only did he watch the tents go up, but he saw acrobats rehearsing and shook hands with many of the performers. His guide escorted him to the dignitaries' box for the first performance and sat the astonished boy in the best seat in the house.

Weldon loved the circus. The crowd seemed especially enchanted by one of the clowns. Weldon was shocked when, in the middle of a routine, this clown came over to the box where he was sitting, leaned casually toward the big-eyed boy, and asked him how he was enjoying the show.

It wasn't until he returned home that evening that Weldon realized that he'd spent his day in the care and company of Emmett Kelly, the greatest clown in the world.

A Taker's Tale

In the eighteen years we've lived in the Santa Cruz mountains, there have been two times when we've been without power for more than a few days. Our first experience was in 1982. Sixteen inches of rain deluged our valley in one afternoon, and the resulting mudslides wiped out whole hillsides. Many lives were lost. When we realized that we could be without power for a long time, we pooled money with a neighbor and bought a gasoline powered generator.

When other neighbors heard the chugging of the generator, they asked to use it. We worked out a schedule for those who asked which allowed for enough power to do a load of essential wash and to rechill their freezers and refrigerators.

Things went smoothly until the Beula's had their first turn with the generator. At the end of their three hours, they loaded it up in their car and took it to their daughter's house for awhile. From there they went to their son's home and then used the generator again at their own house. Then it went back to their daughter's. During this time we had no idea what had happened to the generator. When Randy finally tracked it down, he reminded Mel Beula of the agreed upon schedule with the other neighbors. Mel insisted that the needs of his family were more urgent than the needs of others. When Randy suggested Mel buy a generator for his own family's use, Mel was appalled.

"Why should I spend all that money for something I'll only need once in awhile?" he asked Randy.

What could Randy say to such selfishness? Speechless, he loaded the generator in his truck and brought it home. When we found ourselves without power for four days after the earthquake of 1989, we felt that, for the sake of fairness, we could not offer our generator to the Beula's to use.

All of us are takers at times. *People who make almost every decision based on what they want regardless of the needs of others are takers.* Spoiled children become takers. Those who are praised more for their physical beauty than their inner qualities as children struggle with vanity, a form of taking. Those who have been neglected, abused, or abandoned may become takers to survive the trauma of their early years. All tend to be lonely, negative, and demanding. They have trouble making and keeping friends.

The Cohens are training their children to look for ways to be givers with a game they call *Buttons*. Every Friday night each member of the family is given five buttons of the same color. Mr. Cohen has red buttons, Mrs. Cohen green buttons, Joseph is gold and Sarah is silver. When Joseph does his Dad a kindness during the week, Mr. Cohen gives his son one of his red buttons. When Sarah rakes the lawn without being asked, Mrs Cohen gives her a green button. At the end of the week, each person brings the buttons they've *earned* to the evening meal and the buttons are counted and added to a tally sheet. When the children earn 50 buttons, they go out to dinner with one of their parents.

"How successful has the game been in teaching the children to be givers?" I asked Mrs Cohen one morning.

"Pretty successful," she told me. "Sarah and Joseph not only look for ways to give, they recognize when others give to them." The Cohens' goal is to teach their children the habit of giving. As the children mature, their parents will stop using buttons to motivate them, relying on the good habits and good feelings—the internal motivations—the children have developed.

Finding a Healthy Balance

Carl was a pep leader in his junior year of high school. He volunteered for this job because being in the middle of activities helped him feel popular and liked. The student body counted on Carl to help with major projects. He was in charge of the rallies, homecoming events and dances, and coordinated the transportation of people and equipment for the marching band. Carl gave of his time, creativity, and enthusiasm.

Unwilling to delegate some of his responsibilities, Carl found himself feeling overwhelmed and unappreciated. In spite of his weariness, he hated to say *no* to requests for help. With the endless demands of the junior-senior prom looming ahead, Carl came down with pneumonia. His body finally said *no* for him.

Carl did not know how to recognize the limits of his energy and tried to do everything for everyone. The Yearbook advisor at his school recognized Carl as a *mismotivated giver*. He gave him the following list of things to ask himself before agreeing to take on more responsibilities.

Why do I want to do this?

Is it because of my need for recognition, to be liked, or to take care of others?

Am I staying in touch with and taking care of my own needs?

Am I willing to cheerfully do my best no matter how sizable or simple, how pleasant of unpleasant, or how interesting or boring the task?

Will meeting this need interfere with another commitment?

Am I enabling someone else to be irresponsible?

Am I seeking to love my neighbor as myself?

With the list in hand, Carl learned to set reasonable boundaries on commitments and learned to think carefully before saying *yes*.

Receiving a Kindness or Service

In any relationship there should be a balance of giving and receiving. If everyone gave all the time, there would be no one available to receive the giving offered. Everyone would be exhausted. Therefore, learning to be a gracious receiver is an important friendship skill and a way to give.

Randy had knee surgery in college. His roommate, Rod Stiling, transported him to classes, carried his books, did his shopping, and helped him bathe and dress for the six weeks he was in a cast. It was hard for Randy to be dependent. It was humbling to feel indebted to Rod for his patient care.

Twenty years later they still laugh about their solution to the awkwardness of the giver-receiver relationship: they kept mock bills of services rendered. Rod charged Randy $10 for doing his laundry. Randy charged Rod $15 for borrowing his car. Rod charged Randy $3 for carrying his books. Randy charged Rod $200 for the dent he left in the car's fender. They soon owed each other thousands of dollars. When the cast came off Randy's leg, they celebrated by burning their bills.

Rod still talks about how much it meant to him to really be needed. Randy learned the difficult lesson of receiving gratefully. They both learned the value of humor in uncomfortable situations. Their friendship thrives. Adversity became a building block, rather than a stumbling stone for their relationship.

Receiving a Compliment

Receiving a compliment or an honor can be difficult. When Dawn won the junior high talent show with an outstanding rendition of *The Entertainer* on the piano, she was given many compliments on her playing ability.

"Really, I'm not that good. I didn't deserve to win," was her attempt at a modest reply.

By denying her skill she minimized the years of practice that resulted in her victory. This was unfair to herself. By saying she didn't deserve to win, she questioned the other students' judgment and denied them the pleasure of honoring her talent.

A sincere *thank you* is the simplest reply to compliments. This habit is simply called good manners. Dawn was complimented. She can say "Thank you." By adding, "I'm glad you enjoyed it," Dawn could gently turn the conversation away from herself by showing interest in her friend's feelings. A comment like "That means a lot to me," tells the complimenter that their opinion is important.

To gracefully accept a service, compliment, or honor, express appreciation honestly and briefly. It's okay to express feelings but avoid bragging or comparing oneself to others. "Thank you for thinking of me. I'm thrilled by this honor!" relates one's joy to the giver.

Obstacles to Giving

A major obstacle to learning how to be a giver is the attitude of *self-pity*. Everyone goes through stages of self-pity. Sometimes we relish the attention we get from suffering. When things don't go our way, we feel sorry for ourselves. Moping and pouting commonly occur during self-pity attacks.

This is seen most often in young children. The four-year old who was the last one to get his ice cream cone pouts because he felt he deserved to be first. The six-year-old who has to do her chores before she goes out to play sulks in her room long after her chores could have been finished. A ten-year-old who cries bitterly because his friend can't play with him because his friend is playing with someone else. The thirteen-year-old who missed her ride feels sorry for herself because she has to walk six blocks to school.

These situations will happen. Negative emotions are common to us all. As parents, what action should we take? If we allow these immature attitudes to go uncorrected or reinforce them with sympathy, they become a learned response. If we teach children to deny their emotions, we teach them to avoid facing themselves or their reality. Our children then may find themselves saddled with habits which cause difficulty later in life.

Kahleen Edeal teaches kindergarten. She has many students who do not know how to express their emotions helpfully. They lash out, hit, scream, cry or yell. At every opportunity she trains them to own their feelings but to handle them constructively.

"It's okay to express your feelings," she tells the class. "They are there. They are real. You have feelings but you are not your feelings. You don't have to act on or act out these feelings, and you don't have to hurt other people with them. Dylan thought his table deserved a star on the board for neatness. They did not get one. Dylan could have gone over to a table that received a star and scattered their equipment all over. He could have cried or yelled at me. But he chose to come to my desk and quietly tell me that he was jealous and angry about not getting a star. He used calm words instead of fists. Expressing how he felt helped him feel better and let me know that he is working hard to keep his table clean."

My daughter Laurel and I are reading an old fashioned book called *Pollyanna*. To cope with the poverty of their lives, Pollyanna and her father developed *The Glad Game*, which was played when things didn't go their way. When Pollyanna got crutches in a missionary barrel instead of the hoped-for doll, she and her father decided to be glad that she didn't need them rather than disappointed by the missing doll. They trained themselves to look on the bright side.

When Pollyanna's father died she moved East to live with a sour, lonely aunt. Pollyanna hoped for a room with real carpeting and pictures on the walls, but when her bitter aunt gave her a bare room under the attic stairs she decided to be glad there was a window overlooking the garden. The rest of the book described how Pollyanna and *The Glad Game* transformed her new hometown into a caring community.

I'm trying to teach my children to play *The Glad Game* with allowances for their negative feelings.

"In all situations, we choose our response," I tell them. "We can wallow in self-pity or we can acknowledge the difficulties and our troublesome feelings and then look for the gift hidden in the difficulty."

What happens when I get crabby or upset about things? Any number of young voices remind me, "Just play *The Glad Game, Mom!*"

Complaining

The opportunity to take a group of fourth graders to the roller rink arose one rainy afternoon. Instead of being thankful for something to do, the children complained about everything. There was not enough skating time, no money for candy, someone hogged the video game they wanted to play... I came home convinced I'd never do that again!

My father, who's faced many hardships in his life, often told us, "Complaining is a sign of emptiness. No talent, no self-denial, no brains, no character are required to be a complainer. If you don't have something encouraging or constructive to say about a situation, don't say anything at all."

A great deal of what we see in every situation depends on what we're looking for. Abraham Lincoln said, "Most people are as happy as they make up their minds to be." If we look for the negative, we will always find it. Nothing is perfect. No one is without fault. We can't remodel other people, we can only reshape our lives. To whine and complain about things we cannot change does not bring joy to us or those around us. Being glad for the good things helps us to keep focused on opportunities—not difficulties.

Remember. . .

Giving is finding a need and filling it. Giving includes taking care of our own needs and receiving the appropriate care and giving of others. Everyone can learn to be a giver. Not every service we do for others will be recognized and rewarded, but giving is a wise investment. It yields friendships that will become an unending source of joy.

DISCUSSION QUESTIONS

1. In what areas do you consider yourself a giver?

2. In what areas do you consider yourself a taker?

    How can you work on changing this?

3. What is the difference between a receiver and a taker?

    Give examples of when receiving is appropriate.

4. What do you see as the advantages of learning to give to others?

5. What needs are you aware of that need filling? How could you help meet those needs?

6. Think of a circumstance in which you or someone you were with complained and/or felt sorry for themselves. Did these attitudes help make the situation more tolerable? What attitudes could you or the other person have assumed that would have made the situation more pleasant?

ASSIGNMENT: Think of three ways to give to your family and friends every day this week. This can be with a service, an encouragement, an appreciation, or a cheerful attitude. Notice how they respond to your giving. How do you feel after doing it?

OR—Try playing the Button Game with your family. How did you feel about yourself when you found ways to give to others?

Appreciation and Affirmation

Our local high school girls' basketball team hosts players from around the state for a yearly tournament. When Betsy, one of the teenagers who lived with us was a junior, she asked us to house two visiting players, Tina and Lindsay. In the four days they were with us, we fed them, transported them to games and activities, and made trips to the grocery store to buy the special foods required by Lindsay's diet.

Never once did either girl say *thank you* for the efforts made on their behalf. Betsy was appalled. She attempted to make up for the girls' poor manners by being the one to do the thanking.

"Terry, thanks for making that special trip to the store to buy lunch meat for Lindsay."

"Thanks for taking Tina and Lindsay to their game tonight, Randy."

Betsy hoped her loud and obvious appreciation would remind or influence our visitors to be more gracious. No such luck. The girls returned home after an exciting adventure without ever expressing thanks. Betsy didn't feel like inviting Tina and Lindsay to stay with us the next year.

Appreciation

My friend Joanne has been unable to work for many years due to epilepsy. She lives near poverty with her two children. Her neighbors, Rita and Juan Fernando, spend a lot of time with Joanne and her family. Juan repairs household malfunctions and counsels Joanne during difficult stages of parenting. They take turns transporting the family places (Joanne can't drive.) They care for the children and visit Joanne when her epilepsy requires hospitalization.

In spite of her poverty, Joanne always has a gift for the Fernandos at Christmas. Whether a loaf of homemade bread or a stitchery, it is a token of her gratitude for the care she's received.

Joanne refuses to be a taker. She volunteers to wash and walk the dog whenever she can or, when Rita was bedridden with her fourth pregnancy, Joanne mopped the Fernandos' floors and cleaned their house. Joanne's offerings of thanks encourage Juan and Rita. They find doing things for her a pleasure. Joanne and the Fernandos are models to me of how the give and take of appreciation can work.

Expressing Gratitude

Nathan and his Grandpa Allen both learned another less obvious way to express appreciation several years ago. Grandpa took Nathan to the city to see a show. The show was overbooked and they never got to see it. While they ate lunch their car was towed away and they spent the afternoon tracking it down. At first both Nathan and his Grandpa were grumpy. After awhile, Grandpa turned to Nathan and asked, "Okay, Nath, when life hands us lemons, what do we make?"

"Lemonade!" Nathan replied.

Both the seventy-year-old and the ten-year-old decided to meet disappointment cheerfully and look for the humor in their situation.

"This is great, Grandpa," Nathan said at one point. "How many country kids get to see the inside of a big city police station?"

Grandpa looked up from filling out innumerable forms and laughed. "You're making good lemonade, son."

"Hmm," Nathan hmm'd as they walked with an attendant through an enormous building which housed towed and unclaimed cars. "Instead of hiking through the park or through Chinatown, we get a tour of something most tourists never see—the jalopy jail!"

The car was located at the far end of the building. Grandpa signed the release forms handed him by the attendant. She walked away. Grandpa reached into his pant's pocket and then began patting his other pockets. He lifted a stricken face to Nathan. "You're not going to believe this, Nath, but I seem to have misplaced my keys."

Nathan told me later that he was scared. What if they didn't find the keys? He told Grandpa how upset and scared he was and then took a long, deep breath. "I'll be okay, Grandpa," he said finally. "I really am learning to like huge quantities of lemonade, especially when I get to drink them with you."

The following week Grandpa sent Nathan a "thank you" note. In it he said, *"Dear Nathan,*

Our trip to San Francisco was one frustration after another. I never meant to drag you through what we went through. It was difficult and disappointing, wasn't it? But changing your attitude from grumpy to cheerful was a nice way to meet disappointment. Telling me how much you enjoyed drinking lemonade with me made my day wonderful. It was an unforgettable adventure. Thanks for being such a good sport." Love, *Grandpa Allen.*

Nathan was so touched by this letter that he called Grandpa Allen to thank him. Grandpa took the opportunity to expand Nathan's understanding of the value of appreciation.

"I'm pleased my letter made you feel so good about yourself, Nathan," Grandpa told him. "I hope you can pass that feeling on. All of us like to have our labors recognized. There are many people in your life, Nathan, who would deeply appreciate being thanked: teachers, neighbors, coaches, parents, and club leaders. How often do you go out of the way to make sure that these people know how greatly they are appreciated? Remember, genuine expressions of appreciation can honor, encourage, relieve, cheer, acknowledge, credit, please, benefit, support, and endear those who receive them. That's a lot of blessing in return for a little thoughtfulness!"

Grandpa caught Nathan at a teachable moment and his words had a direct impact on our son. He is better and more creative about saying thanks. Last night he thanked me for fixing dinner, even though he didn't like what was served.

"Thanks for a nutritious and unique dinner, Mom," he told me cheerfully. "I appreciate the fact that I don't have to cook!"

Affirmation

It is sometimes difficult to applaud the accomplishments and virtues of others. The underlining fear is that if they are so good, maybe I am less good. My pride whispers that complimenting someone else diminishes me. Fortunately, this is not true. Compliments magnify the giver. I know I am attracted to people who are strong enough in themselves to honor what is unique about me. Friends who affirm my attempts to grow hold an important place in my heart. I want to offer that to my friends also.

Comparison is not the goal. "You are so thin it makes me look huge," is not exactly positive or affirming. It is a comparison that gives with one hand and takes back with the other by bringing the focus of the comment back to the giver. True affirmations express clear appreciation for someone else.

Affirming our friends lays the groundwork for nurturing, motivating, advising, and comforting your future spouse and children. Marriages and friendships based on affirmations rarely fail. This is a lifelong investment.

Steps in Showing Affirmation

The first step in affirming people is *to acknowledge their presence*. This is why we want our children to greet guests and family members as they come into our home. In fact, we're so old fashioned we require it! It is a way of saying, "You are important enough for me to acknowledge your presence." As we learned in Chapter 4, we testify to the value of those around us by our friendliness.

We affirm friends by *telling them why they are special to us*.

Nathan told his friend Seth that his warm and infectious laughter is something Nathan looks forward to hearing when they are together. Did this statement cost Nathan anything? No. Did it boost Seth's feelings about himself? Yes. Did this affirmation encourage their friendship? Yes.

Alison told her friend Sami that her ability to listen to and understand as Alison expresses her feelings about her parent's divorce shields Alison from depression. Knowing that this aspect of her friendship is vital to Alison, Sami now listens to her with even more care.

Affirming friends includes *recognizing and appreciating their efforts to grow and change.* Learning and applying the friendship skills we are discussing here offers a perfect opportunity for families to practice this.

"Peter, that was a nice job of maintaining a gratitude attitude even when the morning didn't go as planned. I noticed you struggled with disappointment, but didn't complain or get grumpy."

"Patty, thanks for standing by without being asked. You were a big help opening doors throughout the house as we moved the furniture. You found a need and filled it."

My friend Bonnie once attempted to support me through a time of struggle by telling me cheerfully, "You used to be such a complainer, Terry. You're getting better."

Why did this intended compliment depress me? Because the negative reminder of how awful I'd been came first. It would have been easier to hear,

"I know you've been frustrated with a lot of things, Terry. It's good to see you dealing with them without complaining."

Affirmation includes *sharing our friend's dreams, even if they are not our dreams.*

Brett Rill tells of traveling along the coast of Oregon with his Aunt Edith when he was fourteen. At the breathtaking sight of gladiolus fields in bloom, Brett expressed a longing to be a farmer.

"You'd be happy doing that for about a month," Aunt Edith snapped.

He later confided to his Aunt that he was interested in studying physical therapy.

"Why be a physical therapist when you could be a doctor?" Edith demanded.

His final effort to share his dreams with Edith ended after Brett expressed hope that his competitive diving would yield a college scholarship.

"You are too tall to be a great diver," she responded. "You should go out for golf or tennis instead."

Brett knew that he couldn't do all the things he dreamed of doing. But ah, the possibilities! He was young. His idealism wasn't yet limited by reality. Open-minded and enthusiastic consideration of his hopes by Aunt Edith could have been an open door to a deepening friendship. Instead, Brett avoids his Aunt Edith whenever possible.

When Nathan graduates from high school, he dreams of living in the wilderness with his Uncle Steven, a canyoneering and river rafting guide. Steven knows that by the time his nephew is eighteen, riding the white waters may no longer be his goal. But he supports his dream. He sends books on wilderness survival. Nathan studies and takes notes on every detail. Uncle Steven listens to Nathan as he reads off the constantly revised list of supplies he wants to pack along. They discuss the merits and limitations of taking CB radios and canned food with them. Time and maturity will shape Nathan's choices. For now, it is enough to have a place to express his hopes. He feels supported. His ideas are given value.

Everyone dreams. Betty wanted to be a ballerina. What little girl hasn't wanted to be a ballerina? As she pursued this, reality showed her that a tall girl built like a pumpkin on stilts did not have much chance for a career in ballet. Also the training required more work than Betty was interested in investing. But her dream helped to develop some useful qualities such as coordination, determination and persistence.

Betty's parents recognized that their daughter was not gifted in dance. They supported her interest in ballet, but also encouraged her to pursue other talents that promised lifelong enjoyment, such as music and tennis. When reality revealed Betty's limitations in ballet, she had other confidence building activities to enjoy.

Affirming friends involves *supporting their activities*.

Disaster struck the first and only time I was to sing a special song during a school event. The preliminary piano music started playing. My duet partner, Sandy, smiled at the college friends who had come to support us and began singing. I opened my mouth to join her and not a sound came out. I tried again and again. My face flushed with embarrassment. The music forged on. Sandy was forced to sing an unscheduled solo.

Guess who was mortified? My friends graciously tried to comfort me. Vague references to courage and willingness to try were muttered. They promised to tell no one of the incident.

At the time, I wished my friends hadn't witnessed my failure. Thank goodness real friends are those who, when you've made a fool of yourself, don't feel that you've done a permanent job. I did appreciate their support. Days later, when time had put the incident into perspective, we were able to laugh about *The Duet* until tears came.

Randy's Uncle Vic died shortly after the mudslides of 1982 paralyzed our little valley. Travel was slow but not impossible. Randy was busy with work. Our children were small. We had many excuses for not making the two hour journey to Uncle Vic's funeral.

Vic and Josephine, his wife, had no children. Although they never expressed it, they looked on Randy and his brother and sister as their own. Josephine was so hurt that Randy did not attend Vic's funeral that she altered the small bequest to us in her will to reflect her displeasure. Randy and I had never gone through the death of a loved one before. We had no idea that a funeral was that big a deal and we grieved to have hurt Josephine so badly. We learned that lesson quickly.

So I learned and am learning to be there for friends: to cheer for triumphs, bring Kleenex for defeats, visit or call when they are seriously ill or in the hospital, attend weddings and funerals when possible. Friends (and children, I've discovered) don't need unasked for sideline coaches or critics. They need cheerleaders.

Remember. . .

We need to offer affirmations to others. In doing so, we become the kind of friend we ourselves would want. Rewarded behavior is repeated behavior. Affirming your friends' thoughtfulness, kindness, or helpfulness will encourage them to be more thoughtful, kind, or helpful. It's a win-win situation. Everyone benefits. Like a pebble tossed into a calm pond, the rippling effect of affirmation touches the lives of those around us.

DISCUSSION QUESTIONS

1. Name three people who help and support you regularly. After their names, indicate a means of showing your appreciation to them for their services. Try to follow through on this as soon as possible.

   1.

   2.

   3.

2. Practice saying *thank you* in the following ways:

   1.   With your teeth clenched and no smile.

   2.   With a big smile on your face.

   3. With a smile and warmth in your voice. Which *thank you* best communicates appreciation? Which one would you enjoy receiving most? Which one do you think others would most appreciate receiving?

ASSIGNMENT

Think of an acquaintance or family member with whom you have difficulty relating. Watch for an opportunity to affirm this person and do so with sincerity. Does looking for the positive in people change your attitude towards them, or theirs towards you? Continue to practice this and see how the difficulties in the relationship are healed.

courtesy\\`kert-e-se\\ noun: *consideration, coop-eration, good manners, and respect for others.*

Courtesy—The Friendship Glue

The Hardin family invited us to the park at four o'clock for a potluck barbeque to celebrate the last day of summer. We arrived at four, set the table, lit the fire for the burgers and waited for the Hardins to arrive. We waited half an hour before starting a game of frisbee golf. After an hour we put the meat on the bar-b-que before the coals died out. We ate hamburgers and drank soda: the Hardins were bringing salad and dessert. We cleaned up. We packed to leave. At six, the Hardin family arrived, apologizing for being late.

Keidi's friend used our pattern for the gingerbread house which won the school bake-off last year. She returned it with pieces missing. There was no apology or offer to make restitution.

Frank borrowed our son's bike and left it in his driveway. His Dad ran over it. Without admitting what happened, he parked the broken bike in our garage.

Tom invited Nathan to his birthday party. Nathan indicated he'd love to come. Tom said he'd get back to Nathan with the details. Nathan never heard from him.

What key friendship ingredient is missing here? *Courtesy.* Courtesy involves surrounding our words and actions with politeness and thoughtful consideration of others. Courtesy affects friendship.

Being on Time

Our friend Alton began battling cancer at the age of twenty. For years he was in and out of treatment and surgeries. One evening as we sat in our living room playing cards, I asked him how the prospect of death had changed his outlook on the way he spent time.

"I see time as a tremendous gift," Alton told us. "Whatever time I have left I cherish as a little chunk of eternity that God has given me to use for helping others. When I thought I had all the time in the world, I squandered it. Now I hoard time."

"How does one hoard time?" Randy asked.

"For one thing," replied Alton thoughtfully, "through the years I got into the habit of being late for everything. I didn't allow enough time to plan or get ready for things. I let time slip by and then I'd be late for something more important. I think that on some occasions I planned to be late to get that little bit of extra attention that comes with walking late into a meeting or class.

"When I lay in hospital beds waiting for visitors who promised they'd come see me at a certain time, every minute of waiting seemed like an hour. So I hoard time by being on time. I have a cousin who is at least an hour late for everything. I love him, but I don't do much with him anymore. An hour lost is never found." Alton shrugged. "I simply don't have the extra hours it takes to wait for him."

Alton died a year later. His comments forever changed my life. As a parent I am trying to teach my children to be prompt by being on time myself. And establishing priorities to better use my time has taken on a new urgency: an hour lost is never found.

Returning Borrowed Items

Returning borrowed items on time and in good shape is a courtesy vital to friendship. When our boys borrow surfboards from the neighbors, they make sure they return them after they've washed the sand off and let them dry, even if they were wet and sandy when they borrowed them. If anything breaks on the boards while they are in their possession, they repair or replace it.

Money owed to friends should be repaid as soon as possible. Large sums should be repaid with interest. Many relationships have gone sour over money lent and not repaid. *Neither a borrower nor a lender be* is an adage that is meant to protect the financial boundaries of courtesy in friendships.

My children seem to be chronically short on cash. We encourage them to accept alternatives to borrowing when they can. "Satisfy your thirst with a long drink from the drinking fountain rather than borrowing money for soda," we tell them.

We also encourage them to avoid borrowing by finding ways to earn money. Chop and stack wood. Sweep sidewalks. Shovel snow. Wash cars. Babysit. Weed gardens. Walk dogs. Learn to save a good portion of earnings for important purchases—a new bike, a sewing machine, fixing a car. We want them to avoid the kind of borrowing that can hurt friendships.

Keeping Commitments

Keeping commitments and being dependable is an important courtesy. When we agree to do something, we need to get it done to the best of our ability. When our teenagers agree to babysit for someone, they are committed. We do not let them cancel that commitment unless they're sick or find an acceptable substitute. There may be times when other activities look better than babysitting, but young people who are learning dependability know how to keep their commitments.

Laurel agrees to play with one friend. Another child calls with a better offer. But Laurel has committed to the first friend, and that's whom she plays with.

Nathan asks me to type his school report which is due Friday. I agree, *if* he gets the report done by four o'clock Thursday afternoon. He does. Honoring my commitment, I type late into the night. The greatest hope for teaching my children dependability is to value and demonstrate it myself.

Procrastination is the number one enemy of dependability. To procrastinate means *to postpone or defer action*. One of the teenagers who lived with us was good at procrastinating. She was also flunking high school. She asked us for a plan to help her overcome this problem. Together we came up with this list:

1) Start immediately by making a chronological list of everything the project or commitment requires.

2) Get done and check off everything possible as soon as possible.

3) Gather all materials and finalize plans for last minute necessities.

4) Try to anticipate potential last minute glitches such as illness, transportation failure, etc.

It was a great plan. Unfortunately, this gal made detailed *To Do* lists and then left them around the house. She could never find them when she needed them and spent the time she would have been procrastinating looking for the lists...

All of us are undependable at times. Apologizing and making amends when we are undependable helps restore our credibility. When my son Jordan forgets his biweekly dog walking appointment, he calls his boss, Mrs. Cordrey, to arrange an alternate time and volunteers to do it without pay to make amends for his forgetfulness. At nine years old, Jordan is learning courtesy and dependability.

Giving Friends Space

Emotional courtesy in friendships involves *giving friends space to be themselves*. This requires freedom from controlling, manipulating, or exclusion in relationships.

Controlling

We invited eight girls to Keidi's seventh birthday party. Within a few minutes of their arrival, two of the girls, Annie and Sherie, engaged in an all out battle for control of the group. Forget honoring the birthday girl. Forget the planned games and activities. The group had to do what Sherie or Annie desired to avoid loud arguments. The power struggle between these two seven year old girls was a wonder to behold. Before things got totally out of hand, we ended the party and sent Sherie and Annie home.

After Keidi recovered from her party, the family discussed how it felt to have a celebration dominated by those who insisted on keeping events, activities, and emotions centered around themselves. It was a good lesson. Keidi understands that being controlled by others hurts.

There are other types of controllers. Sam, who attended a Friendship Workshop, told me this story:

"I was an Associated Student Body Officer for three years in college. We were an original assortment of students, and we came up with unusual but realistic ideas of things we'd like to do and changes we'd like to try. The problem was our faculty advisor. If we even suggested anything that disagreed with his idea of how things should run, he became very angry and intimidating. It got so that we went out of our way not to rock the boat just to avoid his anger. We began to feel like "yes" men. If we *did* stand up to him and got some sort of compromise from him, he went into withdrawal and didn't speak to us for months. It was emotional blackmail."

Manipulation

Manipulation is the shrewd management of the affairs and emotions of others for one's own purposes. It is a form of control.

Harley was happiest with his friends when he got his way. To ensure this, he would whine, plead, bribe or yell at his friends until they either gave in or gave up. Until Harley learned other friendship skills, he got along best with those who allowed him to take charge.

Insecurity was the root of Harley's attitude. Children need to know that their value as people does not vary when they are wrong, less capable in a particular area than others, or not the star of the show. As Harley became more confident of this in his life, he was able to compromise and be flexible. His friendships improved.

Peg and Ernie Gifford decided they would never go out because their four-year-old daughter Susi cried so much when left with responsible baby sitters. Susi was a pint-sized *pity-me manipulator* who used the *icy silence treatment*, tears, sulking, or pouting to get her way. Her parents taught her to handle life in this manner when they catered to her illnesses or gave in when she become emotional about a decision they made.

As foster parents, we learned that children who have been given little or no control over their environment or the events of their lives have extraordinary needs for security. In order to feel safe, they may seek to rigidly control their own feelings and behavior as well as that of others. Due to their need to be in control, they may become judgmental, intolerant, manipulative, and fearful of failure.

The need to control and manipulate others may also develop in homes where unreasonably stern discipline, perfectionism, immature or absentee parenting, or overindulgence of children is practiced.

To relate successfully to controllers, we need to set firm boundaries. This means we let them know what we are comfortable with in a friendship and ask them not to step over those lines. When they do, we can remind them of our boundaries and hope that the friendship means enough to them that they will stop trying to control us.

Our neighbor Marg had to do this with a friend of hers. Gert noticed aloud that Marg had room on her wall for a bulletin board. Marg wasn't interested. The next time they got together, Gert brought a huge bulletin board and insisted that Marg mount it on the wall.

"She was trying to control me," Marg told us later. "I had to tell her that the decoration of my house was off limits to my friends. She was sure I needed that board and pressed her will quite strongly, but I held firm. To redirect her helpful intentions, I told her I did need help wrapping Christmas presents for my family. She could do just about anything to those gifts and they'd look better than if I did them, so I didn't mind her taking over."

Exclusion

The tendency to be *exclusive* in friendships can begin at an early age. To exclude means to refuse to admit, consider, or include; to shut out or reject. The *best* friend idea needs to be put aside, as it is exclusive. There is no need to rank our friends. We can have many *good* or *close* friends without that final label of *best* friend.

My mother introduced me to this idea when I became friends with identical twins Betsy and Nancy Bauer in first grade. In the way of children, one twin or the other would occasionally ask me which one of them I liked better. Mom advised me that it is a courtesy not to name a *best* friend, but to assure each of them that they were my *dear* or *special* friend.

When Rose moved into our neighborhood, she spent several years bemoaning the lack of a *best* friend in her life. Many girls reached out to her and extended a welcome to her family. They considered themselves her good friends, and were confused by her frustration. When the Platz family moved in, Rose found a *best* friend in Arlene Platz. If she had referred thankfully to her blossoming relationship with Arlene as *another close friendship,* the girls who had spent years reaching out to her would not have felt so instantly excluded.

To avoid being exclusive, we need to encourage our friends to have other meaningful friendships. "My boyfriend (girlfriend, husband, wife, *best* friend) is the only friend I need," puts tremendous pressure on a relationship. No one person can meet all your companionship needs. Different personalities fulfill different relational requirements.

As a teenager, Joanie, Janice, Margaret, Barbara and Kirby were the five girls who ministered to the different facets of my life. Joanie was an athlete. She introduced me to gymnastics, trampoline, folk dancing, and health food. Janice was a year ahead of me in school and went through the stages of growing up with me. She advised, reassured, and inspired me with the wisdom of an elder. Janice also taught me to reach out of my world to serve others through teaching swimming to handicapped children. Margaret was my dog walking companion. She had pedigree dogs, I had a mutt. Together we braved dog shows, obedience trials, the related victories and, more commonly, embarrassments. Kirby and Barbara were my soul mates. We talked about everything. Our hearts touched as we discovered the world of great books, love, injustice, racism, history, and the future.

All of these girls had a special place in my life. I related to each of them on different levels and in different activities. I loved them. They were important to me. Although my relationship with Kirby was the most intimate, I learned to avoid exclusiveness by never naming a *best* friend, and by telling all five how much they meant to me. Slumber parties, bike rides, camping trips, a fancy dinner in San Francisco...all of these were adventures shared by the six of us without rivalry because our friendships were open to all.

Today I tell my children to pray for and seek close friends. When they find them, I remind them that friends can be cherished without being ranked. Being open to friendships wherever they are found allows us to enjoy them in all situations.

Remember. . .

Courtesy helps everyone feel good. When we show that we value other people's possessions, time, energy, and emotions, we are honoring them. Relationships salved with courtesy avoid a lot of friction, clearing the path for deep and abiding friendships.

DISCUSSION QUESTIONS

1. Think of an incident where something was borrowed from you and returned broken or in poor condition. What were your feelings towards the borrower? How could he have handled the situation so as to let you know he valued your friendship enough to be courteous?

2. Are you habitually late to certain activities? Who is affected by your lateness besides yourself? How can you rearrange your schedule and priorities to be more punctual?

3. How do you deal with your friends when they disappoint you by not doing things your way or agreeing with your ideas? Are you able to compromise or accept your differences without pouting or sulking? Are you a master of the *icy silence treatment*?

4. Think of one of your closest friends. How would you feel if he/she proclaimed another friend as his/her *best* friend. How would that affect your view of your friendship with him/her?

You never can tell when you send a word
Like an arrow shot from a bow
By an archer blind, be it cruel or kind,
Just where it may chance to go.
It may pierce the breast of your dearest friend,
Tipped with its poison or balm,
To a stranger's heart in life''s great mart
It may carry its pain or calm.
                                    --E.W. Wilcox

Tools for
Training the Tongue

Grandma Graham began telling my siblings and me a story from the family's past.

"When your Grandpa was a young boy, the West was still a wild place. In the summer of 1889..."

"No! No!" Grandpa interrupted. "The incident took place in the Spring, not the Summer of 1888, not 1889. I remember because 1888 was the year they strung up my Uncle Buck for stealing horses."

Grandma corrected herself and continued. "Your great grandaddy had a big red horse named Ding."

"No! No!" Grandpa interrupted again. "The horse Dad rode was named Bing, not Ding. My horse was Silverheels, by the way."

Grandma frowned gently at her husband. She smiled at us and started again. "One day they rode out to check on a distant forest fire. They rode over a hill and found themselves in the middle of what looked like a war party of young Apache braves. The braves started yelling and ran for their horses..."

"No! No!" said Grandpa with a shake of his head. "It was Blackfoot that was chasin' us, not Apaches."

"Would you like to tell this story, John?" Grandma asked him sweetly.

"No," he answered. "I like jest sittin' here with the kids."

"Then please let me tell it," she said pointedly.

"Okay, okay," Grandpa harumphed.

"So Harold, (that was your great grandaddy's name) on Bing and John on Silverheels headed up Lone Tree Canyon like two streaks of blue lightning..."

"Excuse me," said the deep voice we'd come to expect, "It was Stillwell Canyon. Lone Tree is the next one over."

"John, you're wrong," Grandma said stubbornly. "When we moved back to the homestead in Valier, your Daddy took me out to Lone Tree Canyon and told me this story. I'm sure it was Lone Tree."

The two older folks argued for several minutes. We became restless. Brother Michael stood and headed up the stairs.

"Come back here, Mike," insisted Grandpa. "This is like to be the best story you'll ever hear."

Michael, who was thirteen and at the age of great insight and little patience, told him calmly, "Grandpa, your interruptions don't matter to the heart of the story. You are ruining it for us as listeners and for Grandma as the storyteller. I'll catch the ending some other time." With that, he stalked off.

Grandpa looked at the rest of the us. We nodded our heads, agreeing with Michael. Grandpa was shocked into silence.

"Unfortunately, *Lone Tree Canyon,*" continued Grandma a little smugly, "is a dead end. The Indians soon caught up with Harold and John. They pulled their guns from their saddles and surrounded the unarmed men." Grandma paused here for dramatic effect.

"What happened?" asked my brother Ace breathlessly.

"Why," boomed Grandpa one last time, "they shot us dead, of course!"

With that, he slapped his knees and hooted with laughter. Baffled, we looked at Grandma. She was furious.

"That man can't stand living if he's not the star of the show," she fumed. Rising majestically, she swept out of the room.

We were torn between sympathy for Grandma and anger at Grandpa for ruining the story. A noise on the ground drew our eyes to Grandpa. He rolled on the floor, pounding the carpet with his hands and howling with glee. It seemed unfair to us that Grandpa, the one who caused problems, should be the one to get such enjoyment out of the whole episode. I still don't know how Grandma's story ended.

Words are powerful tools. What and how we say things can build up or tear down a relationship. This truth gives immeasurable power to that tiny entity, the tongue. Wars have been fought, kingdoms have been lost, lives have been consumed, and untold friendships have been ended by harsh, angry, and critical words.

Communicating Affection

When my friend Kari married, I orchestrated her wedding rehearsal. Everything went smoothly until I told her father that before delivering his daughter to her husband-to-be, it was customary for the father to give the bride a kiss and express his love for her.

"It may be customary," he told me curtly, "but we will skip that part of the ceremony. I never kiss my children."

"Never?" I asked in astonishment. "Not even when they were babies?"

"I am a good parent," he informed me stiffly. "My father never kissed me or told me how he felt about me. I turned out okay. I've given my children all the things that a good parent provides—a stable home, travel, a university education, musical training. I paid for Kari's wedding. I think that's enough."

Later I asked Kari if what her Dad said was true.

"Sure is," she told me sadly. "Dad's afraid he'll sound fake when he expresses his feelings, so he never does. It really bothered my sister, Lynn. She asked him to tell her he loved her last Christmas. She begged him to just say it. He refused. She hasn't been able to speak to him since."

Children need to know what their parents think about them in order to feel secure and valued. Friends need the same reassurance. Each kind, uplifting word we offer to our friends strengthens our bond with them. It's easy to invest energy and time in a person who expresses delight in time spent together. We are left dangling by people who never indicate if they enjoy being with us.

We verbally communicate affection in two major ways: one, by expressing our love, and second, by speaking highly of friends to others.

Expressing Love

Seven high school girls and I were sitting on the floor of a friend's garage-become-preschool for our weekly Bible study. As usual, we started the meeting studying an assigned passage and then wandered into an animated discussion about a related topic. The passage was from Proverbs 18:24, *"But there is a friend who sticks closer than a brother."*

"Sophie sticks closer to me than a sister," Cana told us, referring to the girl next to her. "Even though when we were younger our fights were sometimes heard by all the neighbors, we never fought for long. And even now when we argue, I don't worry about losing Sophie as a friend."

"How do you know she'll stick with you if you fight a lot?" Sarah, another member, asked Cana.

"She tells me that she loves me about twice a week, and I know she means it," Cana explained. "And no matter how mad I am when she says it, it always feels really good."

"Do you tell Sophie that you love her?" Rachel asked from across the room.

"I do now," Cana told us. "But at first saying it in those words was too much emotion for me. So I said things like 'Your friendship means a lot to me,' or 'I enjoy being with you.' The more I practiced the easier it became to express affection."

"I always knew what she meant, even if she didn't use the words *I love you*," Sophie said. "Cana was never a *gusher*, so I knew she was sincere."

"What's a *gusher*?" asked Keidi.

"Oh, you know," contributed Sarah from her place by the heater, "A gusher is someone who spouts so much praise and so many compliments that you can't really believe they're sincere about any of them. Like when they say to everyone 'What a fun person you are! You make me soo happy!'"

"Or they say 'Oh, you're sooo smart' whenever anyone answers a question," chimed in Laura.

"Yeah, I have a friend who says 'Isn't she great? I just love her to pieces' as a response to every joke or intelligent comment I make," Rachel told us. "It gets tiring. I ignore her, even when I shouldn't. It's like the boy who cried wolf. When she tries to be sincere, I don't believe her."

"It does feel good to know where we stand with someone," I said. "When Laura was new to our group I didn't know how to read her reaction to us. Was this group helpful to her? Was she enjoying it? Did she feel welcome? Then one day she told me, 'I hesitated to join the study because I didn't know what to expect. But now it means a lot to me and I look forward to the time we spend together.' I was so relieved! Knowing that Laura was comfortable made me more comfortable. I feel closer to Laura, too."

"So, getting back to our verse," summed up Amy, our group secretary, "I've written down these points. To help draw a friend closer than a brother (or in our case, sister), be genuine in expressing affection. Tell friends you admire them, care about them, like them, love them. Let them know where they stand, and that they are valued and loved."

Speaking Highly of Our Friends to Others

When ten-year-old Devon Mok's family moved into his cousin Peter's neighborhood, Devon was surprised and pleased to find all of the boys his age excited about "the new kid on the block". The boys welcomed him and he soon had many new friends.

"Do you like living here?" one of the boys, Matt, asked Devon after he'd been there a few months.

"Yeah, it's great!" replied Devon. "At first I didn't want to move because I knew I'd miss my old friends. I still can't believe how easy it's been to make new friends here. It's great!"

"We all wanted to be friends with you," Matt explained. "Peter said so many nice things about you that by the time you moved here we looked forward to getting to know you."

"That's neat," said Devon thoughtfully. "I kinda thought Peter would want me to himself, especially at first. We've always been close. But he didn't do that. He introduced me to all of you. I was afraid I wouldn't fit in, but Peter really made it easy."

Obstacles to Communicating Affection

Efforts to communicate affection and build friendships can be sabotaged by three troublesome dragon scales: *gossip, correctiveness* and *cruelty.* Shedding these scales involves controlling the tongue. The Apostle Paul, in the New Testament, exhorts: *Let no unwholesome word proceed from your mouth, but only such a word as is good for edification according to the need of the moment, that it may give grace to those who hear* (Ephesians 4:29.) Let's look at the ways that an unguarded tongue can wound and dishonor friendships.

Gossip

A teen-aged boy once complained to me that he had been falsely accused of spreading a rumor. "Sarah told Mack that I told her that his brother Jack was getting into trouble with Wanda. Why would I say something like that? Now if Sarah told Mack that I said Jack was messing around with Regina it would have been the truth, and not a rumor. I would own up to that one."

Gossip is defined as *idle, often malicious talk about others.* Malicious means *with active ill will; a wish to hurt others; spiteful.* Cutting down others, belittling them, discrediting them, talking negatively behind their backs—all these fit into the definition of gossip.

Most of us struggle with gossip. Inner signals that lead to gossip need to be recognized so we can be forewarned and forearmed to combat this tendency. When you are tempted to gossip, it is helpful to ask these questions: Am I talking about others to take attention away from my problems? Is gossiping making me feel more *in the know* or more interesting to those I wish to impress? Have I been wronged by someone and feel that talking negatively about them is a suitable revenge? Am I misplacing feelings of anger or frustration and taking them out on whomever gets in my way?

Gossip hurts friendships. It is not fair. It is usually not honest. Chuck Swindoll, senior pastor of the First Evangelical Free Church in Fullerton, California, has an effective solution: *Think first. Talk less. Start now.*

Correctiveness

Michael taught me an important lesson. When I feel the urge to interrupt a story to correct or make an issue out of unimportant details, I remember Grandpa. He wanted attention for himself. But focusing attention on himself did not endear Grandpa to us or to Grandma. We were torn between fascination listening to Grandma's story and irritation listening to Grandpa's interruptions. The next time Grandma related an incident or told a joke, we waited until Grandpa was out of earshot. Grandpa was the loser in the end.

The recipe for controlling correctiveness is the same as that for gossip: *Think first. Talk less. Start now.*

Cruelty in Our Speech

This year started out to be a very difficult one for Nina Jelowski. Nina is in a sixth grade class with a competitive group of kids who seem to place being cool above everything, including kindness, honesty, and integrity.

One of the leaders of this group, Jilia, wrote Nina a mean and insulting hate letter. When Nina learned who wrote the letter she was devastated. Jilia was her neighbor. They grew up together and attended many of the same activities.

When Nina asked Jilia why she wrote the letter, Jilia giggled nervously and said she meant it as a joke. What Jilia failed to recognize is that *cruelty is never a joke.* Proverbs 26: 18-19 says, *Like a madman who throws firebrands, arrows and death, so is the man who deceives his neighbor and says, 'Was I not joking?'*

Nina had experienced this cruel streak in Jilia before. She remembered car pooling to school with Jilia's mother, Jilia, and another neighbor child, Morgan. Morgan was from a poor family. Although she was always clean, she sometimes wore the same outfit to school two days in a row. When this happened, Jilia taunted her, deriding her clothes and calling her a church mouse. "Jilia!" her mother exclaimed in horror. "We don't talk to people like that!" Jilia smiled charmingly at Morgan and her mother and said, "I was only kidding, Mom." Tragically, Mom accepted these barbs as humor and Jilia did not learn to bind her friendships in kindness.

Jilia's cruel words may have given her a temporary sense of power or control. Or she may have felt that putting Morgan and Nina down was a way to improve her own self-esteem or status. In truth, Jilia's attitude pushed people away from her. As her friendships eroded, and so did her self-esteem. Without knowing why, Jilia felt powerless to influence those around her. Her cruel put-downs did not bring the results she wanted.

There is no place for cruelty in our speech, our humor, or in our actions. Many people make a practice of putting down, name calling, teasing sarcastically, or ridiculing their friends. Many parents do this to their children. The pain and humiliation of cruelty, even if it is passed off as humor, is immeasurable.

Standing Together Against Cruelty

The time to stop cruelty in our humor, speech, and actions is now. My children have developed a hand signal that they use unobtrusively to warn each other when the conversation is dishonoring those around them. This signal is used on me when I blast off unkindly at one of them. They are always right, and I am immediately convicted by my words. By using this silent hand signal they do not enter into a verbal battle with me or argue about the right or wrong of the incident that provoked me. They are simply pointing out that the way I handled the situation was unkind. This helps me recognize the nastiness in my speech, so I can work on eliminating it.

Apologizing, Forgiving, and Forgetting

It is said, "People and automobiles progress by a series of internal explosions." There are times when any two people, no matter how deep their friendship and commitment, are going to hurt each other. Anger and impatience are common to us all. I think regretfully of times when misunderstandings destroyed budding friendships. It is helpful when friends build in an allowance for negative feelings, and develop the skills of *apologizing, forgiving,* and *forgetting*

Although some people believe it is demeaning to humble themselves and apologize, the opposite is true. It takes maturity and courage to admit wrongs and make amends for them.

When we first moved to Mount Hermon, Randy befriended five neighbor boys. These boys adored Randy. They dressed like him. They worked with him when they could. They invited him to their activities.

To get his attention, one of the boys, Mark, tried to put rocks in the hubcaps of our car. He couldn't get the hubcaps off, however, so he stuffed the rocks into the brake pads. When we got in the car on the way to a wedding, we didn't just get the clatter and banging Mark intended. We couldn't drive. Randy had to change his clothes, take off the tires and clean out each wheel well. We missed the wedding.

Mark was terribly embarrassed by what he'd done. He avoided us for a few days, and then arrived at our door with a letter of apology. Of course we forgave Mark! Instead of remembering the trouble he caused, Mark's apology left us with a sweet taste in our mouths. He still holds a special place in our hearts.

We need to remember that apologizing does not estrange people, it brings them closer.

The Authentic Apology

Apologizing is a skill and requires training and practice. It is not enough to look at the ground and mumble out something that sounds like *I'm sorry*. To demonstrate the sincerity of our regrets, we need to address the full scope of the hurt inflicted. This is called an ·*authentic apology.*

The authentic apology has four components:

1) Make a specific reference to the incident —

   "Last night at dinner I said such and such..."

2) Confess the offense and admit you were wrong —

   "I was rude (or selfish or gossiping) and my words were out of line..."

   (Make no excuses for your behavior—take full responsibility for it. This gives the other person room to forgive you without feeling defensive, and to, when appropriate, admit "Oh, it wasn't all your fault. I was partly to blame...")

3) Verbalize your repentant spirit —

   "I feel terrible about it, and will try to avoid doing it in the future.. I don't want this to stand between us."

4) Ask for forgiveness and, if appropriate, seal the reconciliation with a handshake or a hug of peace.

"Will you please forgive me?"

(Sometimes this closure is difficult—the wounded party may not be ready to forgive and may feel pressured to voice forgiveness prematurely. Forgiveness is a process. Healing will begin with steps 1-3. Ask for forgiveness, and then be patient if your friend needs additional time to sort out his feelings.)

Teaching children to apologize authentically takes training by word and by example. With young children, it is helpful for the parents to do the wording and have the child repeat after them.

Dad: "Jordan, I want you to look at Laurel and then repeat after me...Laurel, I'm sorry I poked you in the face with the umbrella... I shouldn't have used it as a sword... I won't do that again... I know I hurt you and I'm sorry... Please forgive me."

When apologizing, the authentic apology format will be most successful. Keeping it simple and clear avoids losing the meaning of the apology in too many words.

Where a major apology is needed, it helps to provide personal coaching for children below high school age. Sending a child off to the other room to make amends with a sibling or friend will probably result in little more than a quick *sorry*. Children need encouragement and on-the-spot training until they realize for themselves the value of apologizing.

Let's go back to Nina's story. Nina's father took the hate letter to Jilia's father, Lester, leaving the problem of dealing with Jilia's actions in Lester's hands. Jilia never apologized to Nina. Fortunately, Nina forgave Jilia and they resumed a guarded relationship.

What happened because Jilia did not apologize to Nina? By allowing her to avoid admitting error and to avoid asking forgiveness, her parents missed a crucial opportunity to help Jilia learn all she could have from this mistake. Courage and humility remained strangers to her. Somewhere deep inside, Jilia hates herself for writing that letter. Apologizing and asking Nina's forgiveness would free her from the burden and embarrassment of this incident.

All of us do offensive things. Accepting responsibility for our actions and making amends are vital bonding factors. Only through expressing genuine regret for our behavior can we clean the slate of the past and build healthy friendships.

Forgiveness

Forgiveness is a gift we receive from friends after we have hurt them by thoughtless words, actions or inactions. *Forgiving* a wrong is giving up resentment or bitterness against an offender and restoring a relationship to health. Both being forgiven and forgiving others go beyond the words of an apology—they require honest reconciliation and letting go of negative feelings.

No matter how perfect a friendship seems, sooner or later someone will be wronged. In an unguarded moment an embarrassing word, a criticism, a disloyalty will wound a relationship. At this point, the offending friend has two choices: he can ignore or deny the pain he caused his buddy, or he can apologize, ask forgiveness, and do what he can to clean and mend the wound so it will heal.

The wounded party also has two choices: forgive the offender and allow healing, or hold a grudge. Forgiving frees the relationship so it can grow. Holding a grudge can, like an abscess, impair joy for living and affect relationships with those around us.

"Jordan," I called out the door one Saturday. "Your lunch is on the table. Please come now before it gets cold."

"Be right there, Mom," he answered.

"Jordan," I said half an hour later, "What are you doing out here? Your lunch is cold."

"I captured this ladybug." he informed me. "It's cute. I like the feeling of little legs crawling up and down my hand."

"Okay," I said slowly. "Can lunch fit into this somehow?"

"I am hungry," Jordan admitted. "But holding this thing takes concentration. I'll move inside, but I can't eat. I might lose her."

"What will the ladybug do inside when she wants to eat?" I asked.

"I dunno," the boy replied. "I'll think of something."

"Phone's for you Jordan," Keidi yelled from the kitchen.

"I can't answer it," Jordan yelled back. "I'm busy."

"It's Wesley. He's asking you to go swimming," Keidi reported.

"I'd like to go swimming," Jordan told me. "But the ladybug is fun, too. What do you think, Mom?"

"Seems to me," I told Jordan frankly, "when you hold onto the ladybug you both lose your freedom. In trapping it, you are also trapped, aren't you? Releasing the ladybug would allow you to be a boy and it to be a bug."

Holding a grudge can be compared to capturing a ladybug. At first, there might be some attention or self-pity attached to being wronged. This may offer entertainment or novelty. Soon however, the burden of being the captor hits. Our minds become consumed by the grudge. Exploring other relationships and moving about naturally becomes impossible.

There is one major flaw in this comparison. A ladybug is cute and harmless. A grudge is not. To carry a grudge is like hauling around a backpack full of rocks. It causes discomfort and makes us angry and ill-tempered. These feelings are exhausting.

Unloading the rocks from the backpack is our choice. It requires an act of will. We strive for willingness to ask for forgiveness or to forgive others who have wronged us. We need to be eager to remove all barriers which separate us from friends. Whatever our role is in an offense, peacemaking should be a priority. Why spend life holding lady bugs or hauling rocks? Let's learn to accept our frailties and those of others and get on with developing the gift of friendship.

Forgetting

Healing wounds caused by wrongs done to us by others requires one more skill—that of forgetting. Forgetting does not, in this context, simply mean erasing the memory of the offense. I tried that. A friend borrowed money and failed to return it on time. As the weeks went by and I needed the money, I badgered him for repayment. I didn't like being the bad guy, but I didn't want to let this slide by. He finally repaid me, apologized and asked my forgiveness for being late. I accepted his apology and forgave him. Then I tried to forget the offense. I was successful to the point that within a year I lent him money again. The same thing happened. I realized that erasing the memory of some offenses was harmful rather than helpful. Further research revealed that forgetting means:

1) *refusing to judge the friend,*

2) *giving up the need to get even,*

3) *continuing to honor the friend in spit of the offense,* and

4) *using discernment, common sense, and experience to set reasonable boundaries which acknowledge weaknesses without punishing friends for them.* (In other words, if you've

learned from experience that a friend has a hard time keeping secrets, don't ask that person to keep secrets.)

Refusing to judge means not criticizing or censuring friends for their mistakes. Too often we keep a running total of the hurts we receive from friends and we limit our regard and affection for them according to that impromptu score. Anger may cause us to dredge up old wounds as weapons to fling at friends. Refusing to judge friends by their past mistakes allows them to learn from their mistakes and grow.

Giving up the need to get even frees us from the anger that comes with the desire for revenge. The Golden Rule does *not* say "Do unto others as they have done unto you." It says "Do unto others as *you would* have them do unto you." This is where we unload the rocks from our backpacks and abandon grudges in favor of health and healing in relationships.

Honoring friends in spite of the offense simply means we love and respect friends just as if they'd never offended us and in spite of areas of weakness.

Remember. . .

It is said that speech is the mirror of the soul. As a man speaks, so is he. Training our tongues to honor others in our speech is a giant step towards mastering the art of friendship. This involves communicating affection, speaking highly of friends to others, avoiding gossip, correctiveness and cruelty, and using the skills of apologizing, forgiving, and forgetting to repair frayed relationships.

DISCUSSION QUESTIONS

1. Read the following statements. What is the speaker trying to communicate? How could he or she have worded their comments to better honor their friends?

    A. "You've been really helpful, Tammy. I guess I love you."

    B. "This is my friend, Sharon. She's the one I told you about who had the nervous breakdown."

    C. "You are so stupid! I can't believe you thought you could be a wrestler. They don't have a wimp league here."

D. "Did you see Letisha try out for Letter Guards? She looked like a baby elephant. What a burn!"

E. "Josh kept bugging me about what you told me. He wouldn't let it alone. I told him the secret to get him off my back."

ASSIGNMENT:

During the week, when the occasion arises, make a sincere apology. If you receive an apology, acknowledge it by thanking the giver and telling him or her how the apology made you feel.

Read the following definition of love out loud every day for at least a week. How does it encourage us to honor each other in our speech?

Love is patient, love is kind, and is not jealous; love does not brag and is not arrogant,

Love does not act unbecomingly; it does not seek its own, is not provoked, does not take into account a wrong suffered, does not rejoice in unrighteousness, but rejoices with the truth;

Love bears all things, believes all things, hopes all things, endures all things. Love never fails.

(1 Corinthians 13:4-8)

expectation \ek-spek-'ta-shen\ noun: *look forward to, the supposition or anticipation of having something occur in what one considers a probable, deserved, or right manner.*

Great Expectations—
Helpful or Harmful?

When we bought our home, the yard was a wilderness. We couldn't afford landscaping but we wanted to get something attractive growing out among the weeds. When Bill Kniffen, the Mount Hermon gardener, brought Randy a sprouted almond seed and asked if he was interested in planting it, Randy was thrilled.

"This wild sprout will bloom beautifully in the springtime but it's not likely to bear fruit," Bill told Randy. "It's what's called a bitter almond."

Randy brought the seed home. As the family gardener, I volunteered to plant it.

"Well," Randy hesitated. "I've never planted *anything* before. I thought maybe Keidi (who was a toddler at the time) and I could combine our ignorance and have a Planting Our First Tree Ceremony."

Randy found the perfect spot and planted the almond seed with all the loving care recommended in the Sunset Garden Book. Keidi watched the proceedings carefully. In the next week she pulled up and replanted the sprout three times according to the Keidi Joy Garden Book. We finally fenced it in for its own safety. To our amazement, it grew.

When I miscarried half way through my second pregnancy, we dedicated the tree to the memory of our tiny daughter, whom we named Amanda. Amanda's almond tree became very special to us. Over the years we fertilized, pruned, sprayed, and watered it. We did not expect almonds, but we were delighted with its health and growth. Ten summers after Randy (and Keidi) planted that tree, it bore a crop of delicious *peaches,*

As parents who thought they'd planted almonds, we think of our children as growing up and bearing a specific kind of fruit. This is our expectation. We tend to hold on to this expectation until it begins to feel like a necessary reality. But what if Nathan grows up to be a stockbroker on Wall Street? Or Ben wants to study gorillas in Africa? What if Laurel chooses a different lifestyle than ours? Will we be disappointed if they don't bear the fruit we planned for them to bear?

When I am able to think wisely, I know Randy and I need to faithfully water, fertilize, set boundaries and, when appropriate, prune the trees that are our children. Our friends need the same treatment— without the pruning. Then, when good fruit appears, we can rejoice, even if it's not what we expected. If Amanda's almond tree can bear peaches, we'd better be ready for anything.

How Expectations Work

We all expect certain things from our families and friends, and they from us. If either party is disappointed, the let down or frustration that results may threaten the relationship.

My junior year in high school I was in charge of selling cookies at the annual carnival.

"Please bake and bring at least four dozen cookies," I instructed the bake sale volunteers. "Arrange them on colorful paper plates. If they look attractive they'll sell better."

I went home and spent two days mixing and molding, rolling and folding dough into fancy cookies. Lining red paper plates with pink doilies, I arranged the cookies on them and carefully wrapped them in plastic wrap.

"Oh yes!" exclaimed the cookie booth crew when they saw my trays. "Let's put these in the middle of the table. Maybe we'll get some customers."

A warning bell rang in my head. "What other kinds of cookies did people bring?" I asked.

"Oatmeal drop cookies," the crew responded in unison.

Sure enough, the table was covered with nicely wrapped plates of oatmeal cookies. I knew that oatmeal cookies take all of ten minutes to make.

"Didn't we talk about bringing cookies that sell well?" the not-very-nice part of me asked Jennie, the booth coordinator.

"Oatmeal cookies are good," exclaimed Jennie defensively. "I don't know how to make anything else. I even went to the store to get fancy paper plates to put them on, like you suggested."

What could I say? My expectations were both poorly expressed and unrealistic. Jennie and the others did their best. I had to choose to be flexible and accept what had happened or to be angry and frustrated. My choice was *un*willing acceptance. I made it a point to be cheerful with Jennie and the others in the booth, but didn't hesitate to tell my tale of woe to my friends who would listen.

I felt very self-righteous about the *Cookie Booth Fiasco* until later that same year when I found myself at the receiving end of another set of unrealistic expectations. It started when my study partner, Lance, became the activities director for the Palo Alto Teen Action Council.

"I'm counting on you to be my assistant." Lance informed me after accepting the position.

My eyebrows shot up. "I'm too busy." I replied.

Lance insisted I attend the first meeting. "It won't hurt," he promised. "You can just sit there and get an idea of what's happening. I need your support. If you're there, I'll be less nervous."

"Okay," I said, caving in. "But don't expect too much."

A few minutes into the meeting I realized I'd been taken. Lance's ideas were wonderful. To convince the steering committee that he could carry out his ideas, he explained that I'd volunteered to work as his assistant and to help where needed.

"Wait a second," I interrupted. "I never said I'd do this, Lance. I don't have time. Tomorrow I'm trying out for the marching band. They practice every afternoon."

Lance flipped.

"How can you desert me when I need you the most?" he demanded. "I told you I was counting on you to help me with this job!"

"You *told* me that, yes," I said, trying to control my anger, "But I never agreed. You weren't listening. I said I'd come here with you for moral support, nothing else. I'm sorry Lance. I can't do it."

With that I walked out of the meeting.

Later, in tears, I talked over both of these incidents with my mother. Her reply stayed with me, because her opening words so aptly described my experience.

"Oh dear," she said sympathetically. "So often I've found that *if we don't learn our lesson by being the windshield, we have to learn by being the bug.*"

"Expectations are difficult," she continued after we finished laughing. "Some expectations prepare us to cope with situations and we need that. Others, like yours with the cookies and Lance's with your time, are not realistic. When we hold onto those we not only set ourselves up for disappointment but we're also being unfair." Mom looked at me. "Since you don't want to lose Lance as a friend, how do you think you'll handle seeing him again?"

I thought for a moment. "I guess it's easier to blame someone else than to see my own part in the problem," I admitted. "Now that I've calmed down, I want to talk to Lance about all this so it won't come between us or happen again."

Realistic, Clearly Expressed Expectations

Mom pointed out a problem I had and still have in dealing with people. I am an *assumer.* I assume that my husband, children, friends and coworkers magically understand what I want and need from them. I'm learning that I must be on the alert for situations in which I decide how people should act, and then become disappointed when they don't fulfill my mental picture but do as they want or as they think best for themselves. This has been particularly true with my children.

Clearly Explain Expectations

"Laurel, if you're old enough to fix your own snacks, you are old enough to clean up the mess you make," I said firmly to my seven-year-old one afternoon.

"I did, Mom," she replied. "I rinsed my plate and put it in the dishwasher." She opened the door to go and join her friends outside.

"Wait a moment. That's only a start," I said. "Come and look carefully. What is out on the counter that was not there before you started your sandwich making?" "You mean the bread? And the peanut butter and jelly? Should they be put away?" she asked.

"Yes," I replied. "And how about the messy cutting board? And the spreading knife and your milk glass? It would help if you'd close all of the drawers and cupboards that you opened. If that blob on the floor is peanut butter, you'll need to wipe that up, too."

"I didn't know I'd have to do all that," Laurel protested.

"I'm teaching you this so you'll know what I expect," I explained. "Otherwise I'll get upset with you every time you fix yourself a snack and leave a huge mess for whoever uses the kitchen next."

"It's not fair! I never had to do all this before!" she continued.

"I know," I said persuasively. "You're old enough now to do your own clean-up. I'm telling you what is expected so we can agree on what needs to be done. When you learn that, I'll feel good about letting you fix your own snacks."

"Oh, that sounds good," Laurel agreed quickly. "Now I've got to think of snacks that don't make a mess..."

Marilyn Miller, the principal of the Mount Hermon Play School is an expert at expectation training. Her example has helped me rethink the way I speak to children. Instead of yelling "Hey Geoffrey, stop hitting Patrick with the blocks," which would be my approach to controlling Geoffrey's behavior, Marilyn takes Geoffrey in her arms. She then says calmly, "Geoffrey, your friend Patrick wants to enjoy his playtime with you. Hitting him with the blocks scares and hurts him. If you think Patrick used some of the blocks you wanted to play with, talk to him about it. We want to keep the block area safe for building."

I've found that the best way to help people understand what we expect of them is to take the time to tell them *before* things start to happen. Obvious as this seems, I've learned the hard way. Not only does a family with six children rarely get invitations to other people's houses, but when we arrive we can overwhelm our hosts with noise and activity. We've learned to express our expectations to the children before we go places in clear and simple terms.

"The Hirsch's have courageously invited us all to dinner, again," I told the kids recently. "Since our last visit was a groaner, let's talk about ways to be more relaxed this time."

"What's a groaner?" asked five year old Ben.

"A groaner," Nathan told him, "is when *someone* opens the gate and lets the expensive dog out of the yard. We groaned a lot in the hour and a half it took us to recapture him."

"A groaner," added Keidi pointedly, "is when a small boy decides to play bomber pilot near the table set with Mrs. Hirsch's china. Luckily, the small boy only knocked over the water pitcher."

"I don't remember that," Ben said innocently. "I must have not been born then."

"A groaner," Jordan continued with a grin, "is when Daddy skips over the first steps from the Hirsch's deck to the yard and jumps right through the bottom step. Mr. Hirsch groaned until he was sure Daddy was not hurt."

"How can we make things different this time?" Randy asked the children.

"I'll put a stick in the gate latch so no one opens it and lets the dog out," Nathan offered. "Or we could leave Ben and Dad at home." He flashed his *gotcha* grin.

"I think we should ask the Hirsches to go over their house rules with us," Keidi suggested. "Maybe rowdy kids could stay outside most of the time."

"And Daddy should bring extra wood and hammer and nails in case he breaks another step," Jordan told us.

"And we all need to remember that the Hirsch's house is small and not set up for children. If we are on our best behavior, I think things will be fine," I assured them. "Let's see, if I point at my eyebrow while looking at you, that means settle down, okay?"

Unrealistic or Unspoken Expectations

Most of us have trouble telling friends what we need or want. Sometimes we don't know ourselves. Sometimes what we want from others is unreasonable. At a recent *Workshop on Friendship,* I asked the participants (even if they were unmarried) what they wanted from children, spouses, and friends. My favorite answer came from Pamela, a young single woman. She said:

"I want well-behaved children who perform outstandingly in at least one area, get good grades, and are well-liked. I want a well-behaved husband who treats me like a priceless treasure, is respected by the community, and is so wonderful that people think I must be pretty incredible for a man like that to fall in love with me. And I want fascinating friends who will recognize how truly terrific I am, will affirm and serve me, and who never forget a special occasion, criticize my children, or flirt with my husband. They must be plain enough to show off my beauty, rich enough to take me to lunch, and of high enough social status to make me feel elevated by their crowd."

Although Pamela later assured me she wrote this as a joke, her words ring of truth. Our hopes and imaginations often combine to paint an unrealistic picture that we expect others to make a reality for us. The best way to bring our expectations down to earth is to talk about them with those involved.

Expecting Others to Make Us Feel Good About Ourselves

One of my college roommates, Jane, spent her childhood trying to make her parents feel good about themselves.

"My parents," she told me, "have never been happy with me. The shrink they sent me to says it's because they went from poverty to extreme wealth in about five years. They tried hard to fit into the rich society in our town. Unfortunately, that included pushing my sister Mary and me into activities that would reflect high society glory back to them.

"Mary loved it. She's pretty, smart, and loves social events. I've always been shy, plain Jane. My folks wanted me to be beautiful. They had my nose and teeth straightened, a plate put in my chin so it wouldn't recede, and my ears surgically pinned flat. They constantly worry about my hair and my weight."

"Gross," I exclaimed. "How could you stand it?"

"It's been painful, in more ways than one," she told me. "To top things off, I had to be a debutante. I didn't want to but they promised me my own car if I went through with it. I had no boyfriend. Dad paid a neighbor's son to escort me. Believe me, it was humiliating."

"Has being away from your folks made it easier to be yourself?" I questioned.

"It's been great! Why else would I pick a college as far away from home as possible?" Jane chuckled. "But when I go home the same old message is there: *We need you to show us off as parents of outstanding children. We are not happy with you unless you are beautiful, smart, or socially desirable.* When I graduate, I'll probably stay out here and never go home."

Failing to Make Our Expectations Clear

Randy had a different experience with expectations. He remembers yelling crossly at his Mom:

"Mom, where did you put those summer camp brochures that were on the coffee table?"

"You mean the ones that have been laying around the house all winter?" his Mom queried. "I finally threw those away. Why, did you need them?"

"Need them?" Randy sputtered. "I was leaving those brochures around the house for you and Dad to discover. I wanted you to look through them, ask me if I was interested in summer camp, and then agree to send me."

"I think you forgot something, Randy," his mother said. "We're not mind readers. You could have just come out and told us what you wanted. I had no idea you were interested in camp. I thought the brochures were junk mail."

A few days later, Randy brought his mother a new brochure.

"Look, Mom," he said with a salesman's enthusiasm. "This is a camp brochure. Camp is good for kids. It teaches them new skills and independence. I would love to go this summer. Do you have any questions?"

"Good job," his mother said. "I get the hint. However, I don't think I heard anything about the price..."

Expecting People and Events To Conform To Our Expectations

Expectations that are too high aren't the only problem. Sometimes we get into trouble because we have negative expectations.

When my honorary aunt and uncle drove their nine-year-old son Martin up to visit his penpal's ranch in northern Nevada, Martin was horrified.

"Writing to Erin is one thing," he protested. "Visiting is quite another. Erin is a *girl*. I don't play with girls. She's also deaf and talks funny. This'll be a boring vacation!"

"No thanks," Martin said, turning down every activity offered in the first three days of his visit. "I think I'll stay inside where it's cool and read magazines."

"Come and see," Erin urged Martin on the morning of the fourth day. "My ewe has newborn lambs."

The excitement of the birth brought Martin out of his personal pity party. Within hours he was enjoying life on a cattle ranch.

"You know, Erin can rope a calf, saddle and ride a horse, and handle a rifle," he confessed to his father. "And she's pretty easy to talk to. I just have to slow down and let her see my lips. We're going to ride out to the Hot Springs before dinner. Wow! This has been the best day of my life!"

The fifth day Martin and his folks loaded the car and drove home.

"I'm so stupid!" Martin groaned from the back seat. "I can't believe I missed so much!"

Maintaining Fairness in our Expectations

How do we make sure our expectations are fair? The key is to learn to *negotiate* what we expect other people to do for us.

Lance and I talked about expectations several days after his first Palo Alto Teen Action Council meeting. He apologized. I apologized. Our friendship resumed. Several months later the Action Council found itself at odds with the adult steering committee on how to spend money donated for activities. In 1968, students seemed to react radically to everything *establishment,* and what seemed to be a small disagreement became, with media attention, a major battle.

In an attempt to calm things, a school counselor agreed to help both sides talk together and work towards finding an agreement. This is called negotiating. Mr. Lomax, the counselor, explained that, in addition to abiding by rules of courtesy when discussion was opened up to the people, we were to keep in mind the suggestions written on a huge blackboard. These spelled out the expectations for both sides. If we followed those guidelines, we were welcome to participate in the meeting. They were:

1. *Each of us will make a special effort to consider the needs of the student community as well as the steering committee. We hope to come to a compromise that will benefit both.*

2. *We will be honest in asking for what we want. No hidden agendas.*

3. *We will request rather than demand changes. We will try hard to understand both sides and meet everyone's needs.*

4. *We will be ready to compromise when necessary. We are aiming for a win-win agreement.*

5. *We (the students) want to clarify what we need, not to manipulate or control the steering committee. We (the steering committee) want to clarify what we need, not manipulate or control the students. Both of us will ask ourselves, after we've worked hard to understand the whole picture, whether our requests are reasonable for all affected.*

With a little coaching from Mr. Lomax, we followed the suggestions carefully. As a result, we left the meeting with a preliminary agreement for a new budget. I left with a new understanding of the value of negotiation in meeting people's needs and solving problems.

Randy learned the value of negotiation when he wanted to go to camp. He explained his desires carefully and clearly to his mother. She understood his request but admitted finances were a problem.

"It's only $400 for the three week session," Randy wheedled. "I could save my allowance to help pay for it!"

"Let's see," his mother calculated, "if you saved from now until August you might have $20. But look at this," she said, taking the brochure from him, "there is a one week session that only costs $150. If you put the money you were saving for drums with your allowance and any other money you earned by doing odd jobs for the neighbors, you could probably come up with $75. That's half. If Daddy and I paid the other half, would you be happy going only one week?"

"Well," Randy hesitated.

"I'm afraid that's the best we can do, son," his mother spoke softly. "Otherwise, you could start saving for the longer session now and plan to go next year."

"A week sounds great," Randy compromised with a whoop. "Thanks Mom!"

Don't Forget to Consider the Intention of the Heart

At times I as a parent focus too intently on obedience and end results without regarding the intention of the heart which may have prompted my child's behavior.

Years ago a sixteen year old foster child, Dee, was assigned to clean the bathrooms as one of her chores. She noticed that the walls were dirty, so she sprayed them with a strong tub and tile cleanser and then went to her room to read while that soaked in. Wails were heard throughout the house when Dee returned to her task to find the paint and wallpaper peeling and streaked. I reminded myself firmly that in spite of the hours of work Dee's efforts caused, her intention was to be helpful.

One night our oldest son did not come home until very late. We were worried and angry by the time he showed up. His excuse? His friend Hugh's little brother died recently. This evening the two boys sat at the park and grieved. Nathan felt that being with Hugh at this time was more important than being home on time. Our reaction to this situation was tempered when we considered the intention of Nathan's heart. We found it helpful to remind ourselves that *"God does not see as man sees, for man looks at the outward appearance, but the Lord looks at the heart."* (1 Samuel 16:7.)

Personal Loving

There *are* healthy ways of trying to meet the reasonable expectations of our friends. I call this *personal loving*. Personal loving is *loving someone as they desire to be loved*. This concept is derived from St. Paul's letter to the Philippians (2: 3, 4): *Do nothing from selfishness or empty conceit, but with humility of mind let each of you regard one another as more important than himself; do not merely look out for your own personal interests, but also for the interests of others.*

Keidi had a secret admirer when she was in eighth grade. Almost every day a small bunch of hand picked flowers appeared on our doorstep with her name on a scrap of paper tied to it. The flowers were the delight of her mornings.

These feelings diminished by the afternoon, however, when we carpooled to swim practice. One seven-year-old in our carpool, Jon, was constantly late. Waiting for Jon to find his suit and towel became a daily frustration, particularly for Keidi, who liked to arrive at the pool early.

One morning Keidi's admirer was late delivering the flowers and Keidi caught him in the act. It was Jon.

"Why do you bring these every morning?" she asked abruptly.

"A commercial on TV says that flowers say *I love you*," Jon chirped, blushing a deep red as he realized what he'd said.

"Jon," said Keidi carefully, "I like you. I enjoy babysitting for your family. I appreciate the flowers. I mean, I'm really flattered. Thank you. But the good feelings the flowers give me are erased by the frustration I feel when we are always late for swim practice. I'd like it more if you were ready when we came to pick you up."

Jon got the point. Keidi had explained what would make her happy. Jon wanted to preserve Keidi's opinion of him. He made every effort to be ready for swimming for the rest of the summer. Keidi realized she could have talked to Jon about his lateness at the beginning of the summer and avoided a lot of disappointment and hard feelings.

My son Jordan enjoys woodworking. He'd rather cut and hammer and sand in the garage than do his chores.

"Jordan, this is the third wooden boat you've made me this week. I love them, but why do you give them to me rather than playing with them yourself?" I asked him one day.

"Because I love you, Mom," he told me.

"Thank you, honey," I said. "I love you too." I added with mild exasperation, "Did you ever think that I might feel more *personally loved* if you worked less on your building projects and did your chores without being nagged?"

"No, I never did think that, Mom," he told me frankly. "Are you saying I should try harder to get the chores done before I head for the garage?"

"Exactly!" I answered with a smile.

Personal Loving Requires Communication

We need to know and understand our friends in order to love them the way they want to be loved. This involves getting to know their interests, likes and dislikes, whims and fancies. Friends know from my house decor that I collect Noah's Arks and angels. They personally love me when they pick out cards or gifts reflecting these interests on my birthday or other holidays.

We encourage the children to be aware of the special interests of their friends. Keidi knows that her friend Amy Larson collects elephants, and is on the look-out all year for unusual elephant gifts for her. Our Nathan and Hugh Christianson spend a lot of time planning outdoor expeditions. Camping gear is always a welcomed gift for

Hugh. Jordan and his friends James and Wesley play rollerblade hockey every afternoon. Since they're always losing the balls in the woods, Jordan doesn't have to think twice about what to get them for their birthday gifts. There are many times when I come right out and ask how I can best express love to my friends or my children.

"Would lunch at a nice restaurant or a surprise gift be more fun on your birthday?" I might ask. The older children usually opt for cash. That's fine with me. I want to personally love them in their gifts.

When my elderly neighbor, Margaret Cordrey was widowed, I asked her how I could most help her. I suggested help with meals, gardening or shopping.

"Could I stop by your house once in awhile when I feel the need to talk with someone besides my dog?" she asked.

"Of course!" I answered. That need would not have occurred to me. Years have passed. Margaret stops in often and has become a dear and treasured friend to all of us.

Remember. . .

Expectations can be constructive. Reasonable expectations give relationships a framework of courtesy and understanding. Expectations become unreasonable when they are unspoken, rigid, inappropriate, or self-serving. We must learn to replace these with fairness, honesty, and two-sided negotiations so we can reach a compromise that is fair to both. Friendships then become comfortable and long-lasting.

DISCUSSION QUESTIONS:

1) How do the following statements put expectations on us? What kind of responses would move these expectations into open communication or negotiation?

   a. "If you really want to be my friend, you'll have to play with just me at recess. I'm unhappy when you try to include other kids in our games."

   b. "I'm sad. I need you to cheer me up."

   c. "Please stay with us while your family is on vacation. If you go with them, I'll be lonely."

   d. "It was a lot to ask when I hired you to babysit five young children, especially since two of them are sick. But I really did hope you'd find time to clean the house. I haven't been able to get to it."

e. "Why should I put up all of my collectibles just because you're bringing a sixteen-month-old child to spend the weekend?"

f. "Wait a second. You knew six weeks ago that this report was due tomorrow and you haven't started working on it? Now you want me to take you to the library and then type up a minimum of twenty pages when you get done tonight?"

g. "You don't want to try out for the football team, Davey? But you're the biggest kid in the school. You'd be the star!"

Note to Parents: Listed below are suggestions of reasonable and appropriate expectations parents and children can have of each other within the realm of family life.

IT IS REASONABLE AND FAIR OF PARENTS TO EXPECT THEIR CHILDREN TO:

1. Treat themselves and others with respect and consideration.

2. Take care of their possessions and the possessions of others.

3. Be aware of and honor family values. This may include boundaries set on dating, driving, curfew, types of television programs watched and music listened to, acceptable language, church participation, drinking and drugs, etc.

4. Keep up with school work, chores and other responsibilities to an agreed upon level.

5. Participate in increasing levels of *independent living skills* as they approach adulthood. Shopping, cooking, laundry and mending, managing money, arranging their own transportation, holding a job, and making their own dental and medical appointments are examples of skills that benefit young adults before they begin living away from home.

IT IS REASONABLE AND FAIR OF CHILDREN TO EXPECT THEIR PARENTS TO:

1. Treat themselves and others with respect and consideration.

2. Take care of their possessions and the possessions of others.

3. Honor and model family values with the goal of a healthy lifestyle for all members.

4. Meet their children's reasonable needs for physical, emotional and spiritual health and growth.

5. Train their children in independent living skills as they are able to successfully assume responsibility.

My friend,
As we progress on the road of life,
I will be there for you,
To walk with you in the way,
To stand beside you in battle,
To rejoice when you rejoice, and
To weep when you weep.

Loyalty in Friendships

As We Progress on the Road of Life

My brother Ace and his friend Gordon went all the way through school together. They were were close buddies until high school, when Gordon began hanging out with guys who were into drugs. Ace was devastated by the change in Gordon. "Come on, Gordon, we miss having you over. I miss studying with you. What do you like about drugs, anyway?"

"I'm travelling a different path now, Ace," Gordon told him his eyes gazing at a distant vision. "It's opened up my mind. You really ought to try it."

"You're travelling a dangerous path," Ace warned his friend. "Count me out. Drugs scare me. It can't be that great. Come on, Gordon!"

Ace's pleading had no effect. After three months of watching Gordon self-destruct on drugs Ace realized he had nothing in common with his friend anymore. Gordon refused to even speak with him.

Gordon finishes the story as he told it to my children at a class reunion picnic:

"When I entered a drug program in our senior year, Ace overheard the guys I hung out with putting me down for trying to get clean. Ace felt sorry for me. I think he understood how lonely I was feeling.

"Ace visited me weekly during the three month program. He was the only one who did. He stood by me through all the garbage that a junkie goes through when they withdraw from drugs. I was in pain. Your poor uncle took a lot of my anger, but he kept coming back.

"I once told Ace that I didn't deserve a friend like him. Ace said he saw me getting better and he stuck with me, thank God."

"Why did you stop being friends in the first place?" asked one of my younger children in confusion.

"Ol' Uncle Ace did the right thing," Gordon said, speaking directly to the teenagers in the group. "If he had stuck with me into drugs he wouldn't have been in shape to help pull me out. The important thing is, when I was ready to change, Ace's loyalty brought us back together."

To Walk with our Friends in the way

Life happens daily. It isn't always exciting. Friends who listen to and help us deal with the routines of life are expressing loyalty.

When Jason Rollis transferred to a new junior high school, he used his gift of making people laugh to make friends. He soon gained the reputation of being the class clown. Although he was included in social activities, he felt as if his classmates looked to him for entertainment. When he was not being amusing, no one was interested in him.

Jason worked on being a loyal friend. He asked other students about themselves and listened attentively to their answers. He made a point of remembering what they were concerned about and asking them specifically about these concerns. Gradually, Jason's interest in the daily lives of the others convinced them that he was more than a clown. He developed meaningful friendships.

Ebbs and Flows in Friendships

In walking with friends in daily life, we must be aware that relationships go through periods of activity and inactivity. I call these the *ebbs and flows* of friendships. There are many factors involved in this, including *physical proximity* (when Jordan's friend Ben Somerville moved out of our neighborhood, their friendship became less active), *the changing of ties that define the friendship* (when Devon dropped out of Nathan's basketball team the boys lost the activity that held their friendship together) and *personal growth needs* (when Keidi's friend Romina went to college, she left good friends who were still in high school but she needed time and energy to make college friends, causing an ebb in her old friendships.)

When we learn to accept the ebbs and flows in friendships, we experience less jealousy or guilt when a relationship is inactive. Ebb times are a reason why it is important to have more than one meaningful friendship. When one friend can't be there for us, another can.

Loyalty through ups and downs has been demonstrated by Keidi's friendship with Amy Larson. These girls are ten months apart and have known each other all of their lives. Over the years, their friendship has fluctuated in closeness and enthusiasm. However, they've stayed in touch and have been unfailingly friendly during the ebb times. They've worked through problems that have arisen, and have always *been there* for each other in times of need.

During Keidi's sixth grade year, she and Amy were very close. The following year Keidi went into junior high, where a different school and different experiences caused things to ebb. Now, throughout the fluctuations of their high school activities, they have stayed in touch, remained unfailingly friendly, and have done what they could to help each other realize their goals. Keidi has also learned that when someone else can meet Amy's needs better than she can, Keidi can be most helpful by encouraging Amy to invest in the new relationship.

To Stand Beside Our Friends in Battle

When I was in third grade and my sister Deborah was in second, she was *best friends* with Daphne and Liz. For unknown reasons, they turned against her. Because in those days everyone at our school belonged to "clubs," Daphne and Liz formed the *I Hate Debby Club* and got many of the girls in their class to join.

Deborah became the victim of these bullies. She received nasty notes and mean phone calls. She was ignored. She was teased and ridiculed. The rest of us Allens were aware that something was wrong. Deborah was sick every morning before school. Her teacher reported that she begged to stay in the classroom during recess. Unfortunately, Deborah was unable to tell anyone what was going on.

One day, I went out to recess to find a large crowd of second grade girls milling around someone on the playing field.

"Why's your skirt yellow, freckles? Did you pee your pants?" I heard Liz yell.

"Don't think you can get away," spat Daphne. "You're going to sit here until we're done giving you a piece of our minds!"

To my horror, the tormented child was Deborah.

I couldn't stand it. Wading into the center of the mob, I fought off those who tried to keep me out. An unintentionally well placed elbow knocked the air out of Daphne. She sat down with a thud. While the others were distracted, I grabbed Deborah by the arm and pulled her out of the crowd.

Deciding adult support was needed, I left my sister in the care of my friends and wrote a note to Deborah's teacher. It said, in large, school-girl printing with several erased and corrected words,

"DEAR MRS. ELKINS, PLEASE TELL THE GIRLS NOT TO BE MEAN TO DEBBY ON THE PLAYGROUND." I signed it, "MRS. ALLEN."

Very graphically, I stood beside Deborah in battle. Although my hostility level was undoubtedly counterproductive, I *did not remain neutral* and allow her to bear this attack alone. Remaining neutral when she needed help would have been the same as abandoning her.

Rescuing friends from physical harm is not usually required when we stand beside them in battle. We cannot fight their emotional or spiritual battles for them, but we can strengthen them with support, encouragement, and prayers.

To Rejoice When Friends Rejoice

Four of my close friends and I applied to spend our senior year of high school abroad with the American Field Service Program. Only one of us could go. The fierce competition left us tense and irritable. I was selected.

The tears shed by these friends over their disappointment didn't keep them from rejoicing with me. They took me out to lunch at a fancy restaurant and had the waiter serve an enormous cake which said, in pink icing, *We're Proud of you, Terry. Congratulations!* That luncheon was one of the greatest honors I've ever received.

To Weep When Friends Weep

When Harley first came to live with us, he went through weeks of homesickness that were hard for neighborhood children to understand.

"You shouldn't be sad, Harley," they'd say, "You've got a good home now."

"I know," said Harley sadly. "But I still miss my folks."

One day he climbed into my mother's lap, told her how sad he felt, and burst into tears. Mom held this hurting child on her lap and grieved with him.

"This must be very hard for you, Harley" she agreed. "Of course you miss your parents. I'm so sorry this happened to your family. I hope they'll get well and you can be with them soon."

"You mean I'm not crazy to be sad?" Harley asked.

"You're not crazy," she assured him. "Missing your folks is normal. I'd be worried if you didn't miss them."

Mom and Harley sat together for several minutes. Harley smiled at Mom, got down and went out to play. His feelings had been understood. Having someone take the time to understand his grief made his burden easier to bear. Homesickness was never a serious problem for Harley after that.

It is easy to weep with a friend whose grief we share. It is when we do not understand why friends are sad, or feel that they should not be sad, that we need to make every effort to take their sorrow seriously and not measure it by personal feelings. Their experience does not have to fit into our experience.

The phone rang. Muffled sobs were all Randy heard when he answered it.

"O'Malley died," the caller gasped.

Randy caught his tongue. O'Malley was the elderly poodle of our impoverished friend Kathleen. Over the past few years, we watched Kathleen shell out hundreds of dollars for medical treatment for O'Malley while her own children went without gifts on birthdays and Christmas.

Randy is not a pet person. He was relieved O'Malley was gone. How could he address Kathleen's sorrow when his feelings were so different from hers?

The solution was to address her emotions, not Randy's. After a long moment of thought, he said, "I'm so sorry Kathleen. I know you'll miss him. He was part of your life for a long time. It's okay to cry."

Remember. . .

To progress means to move forward. Loyalty to stagnant, unhealthy relationships isn't good for anyone. There is a time to let go of friends who are hurting us. Unfailing friendliness and respect will keep doors open for what may become a positive relationship in the future. Healthy loyalty occurs in friendships where both parties are growing and maturing and able to encourage each other to reach their greatest potential.

DISCUSSION QUESTIONS:

1. Can loyalty go beyond the point of being healthy for all parties involved in a friendship? When?

2. Your friend Judd finds the master key to a nearby hotel. He suggests that you and he break into the office and help yourselves to the candy supply there. Remembering that loyalty builds and strengthens the good in friendships, what will you do as a loyal friend when:

   -Judd calls you a coward and a baby for not joining him?

   -He offers you stolen candy and hints that there's more where that came from?

   -Judd stops associating with you, and ridicules you when he sees you?

-You get a call from Judd, who is in jail. He is terrified. He apologizes for hurting you and admits that he was wrong. He asks if you will consider resuming the friendship.

3. Think of a friend you have been very close to but are now not spending much time with. List the reasons for the *ebb* in the relationship. What can you do to keep the door open for a *flow* time in the future?

4. When good or difficult things happen to you, which friends do you turn to? How do these friends express their joy at your joy or sorrow at your sorrow? What can you learn from their loyalty?

whole \`hol\ adj: *in sound health, not diseased or injured; not broken, damaged, immature, or defective; complete or intact: holy.*

Encouraging Each Other to Wholeness

Joseph and his family lived in Florida in the early 1800's. Their farm covered flat plains of marshy grasslands alternating with rolling hills. Every winter, birds of prey, including bald eagles, migrated to the outcroppings of rocks around the farm and laid their eggs. Joseph and his friends were allowed to spy on the eggs and occasionally handle them, for it was known that birds of prey did not defend their eggs. Only when the young birds emerged did the adult birds protect them.

The boys loved to hold the eggs for they contained a mystery and power-yet-to-be that enthralled them. Keeping the eggs was strictly forbidden. The boys knew that a falconet or an eaglet would soon hatch from the eggs and grow quickly into a demanding, dangerous pet.

One winter Joseph became particularly entranced by the allure of the eggs. He broke the family rule and took an egg home, hiding it in the privacy of his tiny bedroom.

"Baby birds are so harmless," he told himself.

Soon the egg hatched. Out came an awkward, bare, unsteady, pathetically adorable baby eagle. Joseph fell in love with it. Though he knew it was prohibited, he kept the eaglet. "Maybe this one will be a good pet," he thought.

At first, taming and raising the eagle was challenging and fun. However, the bird soon became noisy and adventuresome. As the weather improved, Joseph found excuses to sleep with it in an unused barn. His school work, his chores and his friendships suffered as the eaglet became more demanding of his time and energy. He spent his free time hunting for mice and rodents to feed the hatchling. He worried constantly about his secret being discovered.

The bird grew steadily. Joseph found he had less and less control over it. It began hunting for prey amongst the barn animals. "What if Dad asks about the strange disappearance of the barn cat's kittens?" Joseph asked himself.

When Autumn came, the eagle was almost full grown. Joseph dreaded being the target of his pet's short practice jumps. The loft stank. There was nothing worse than waking up to the sights, sounds, and smells of an eagle devouring its dinner. Joseph was no longer happy. He was too proud to admit he'd disobeyed, and too ashamed to admit how far out of control things had become.

One morning Joseph awoke to find his worst nightmare realized— his small, tame eagle had grown into a big, wild beast. He had cornered Joseph's baby brother, Thomas, and was swooping towards him, talons extended.

When Joseph tried to get him to fly away, the eagle turned on him.

In desperation, Joseph cried out to his father for help. Within seconds the farmer was there, placing himself between the children and the crazed eagle.

"Kill it!" Joseph screamed, pointing at the bird as it flew back for a full attack. Armed with a shovel and a pitch fork, Joseph and his father battled the boy's pet. Finally, they scared it away for good, but not before they were bleeding and wounded by the bird of prey Joseph had loved.

Lessons from Birds of Prey

In this story, birds of prey are destructive, negative habits. We start by taking into our lives things such as using drugs or alcohol, cheating, stealing, vandalism, pornography, jealousy, bitterness, swearing, sarcasm, and lying. These are little *fascinations* which we have trouble defining as problems. They grow out of control until they dominate our lives.

Birds of prey affect relationships because *they become the focus of energy and attention.* Joseph spent all his time protecting the secrecy of his forbidden pet. He became self-absorbed and isolated from former friendships. The nature of the creature who hatched out of that entrancing egg forced Joseph to neglect those who cared about him.

Often, we become owners of one or more birds of prey. When we do, we are disabled in our ability to help others to wholeness. Birds of prey hurt those around us, even if it seems that we're only hurting ourselves.

Keeping Birds of Prey from Entering our Lives

From the time they were little, all of my children have been given ample opportunity to get in trouble. Sometimes they led their friends into mischief, and sometimes they were led astray by their friends. By the time they were old enough to face serious consequences because of their choices, Randy and I were old enough to realize we didn't have a clue how to help. Providence and our school district provided a class called *Parenting for the Drug FREE Years.* This course taught us how to teach our children *refusal skills* when they are tempted to participate in trouble.

The teaching was done in the form of a role play during the third class meeting. Nathan was asked to pretend he wanted to befriend Eric, even though Eric was known as a troublemaker.

According to the script, the first time Nathan suggested doing something together, Eric's planned activity sounded secretive.

"Let's walk down the creek, all the way to the end where there are no houses and no one can see us," Eric suggested.

Nathan studied the skill sheet and pulled out Skill 1, ASK QUESTIONS.

"What are we going to do there?" he asked Eric.

"Well, my brother gave me some cocaine, and I thought that'd be a good place to get high," replied Eric.

Nathan then employed Step 2, NAME THE TROUBLE.

"That's possession of an illegal substance. It's against the law. Doesn't that bother you?" he asked.

"No, that doesn't bother me," Eric retorted sarcastically.

Unbowed, Nathan plowed on to Step 3, IDENTIFYING THE PERSONAL CONSEQUENCES. The teacher reminded Nathan to refer only to himself, thereby avoiding putting down or accusing his friend.

"If I did that, I could get caught and hauled to juvenile court. I'd lose a whole bunch of privileges and my family would have a hard time trusting me again. Besides, with my luck, I'd become an addict. I don't want to get into that kind of trouble."

Before Eric could turn and walk away, Nathan plunged into Step 4, SUGGEST AN ALTERNATIVE.

"The pool's open this afternoon. Do you want to go swimming with me?"

"Nah," came the reply. "I'm not much of a swimmer."

"You don't have to be in this pool," said Nathan, trying to sell his alternative plan. "You can stand up all the way across. It's hot. The water will feel great. And, it's free." Then, using Step 5, LEAVING THE DOOR OPEN, Nathan ended with, "If you change your mind, give me a call, okay?"

"Yeah well," his friend replied slowly. "I'm glad you still want to do something. Swimming sounds cool. Let's go."

The class applauded the actors enthusiastically. It all went so smoothly in practice. Although only time will tell how the children do in real life, we were relieved to know that they were given tools to work with when faced with this kind of situation.

Sometimes preliminary refusal skills are not enough. *Parenting for the Drug FREE Years* suggests following these guidelines if someone pressures you so much that the skills listed above don't work.

1. Keep calm.

2. Say the person's name and pause.

3. Say "Listen to me," and wait again.

4. Continue using the skills: *ask questions, name the trouble, identify the consequences, suggest alternatives.* If all this fails, walk away. If a stranger or a bully tries to get you in trouble, say *no*, get away, and tell someone who can help.

We are teaching these skills in family meetings and have even tried acting out difficult situations. Though the kids call these sessions *Melodrama Meetings*, we are betting that they will be better prepared when trouble comes.

Randy also tells the children that knowing who they are and where they want to go in life will help them make healthy choices. (More about this process is coming in Chapter 13.) Randy speaks from personal experience.

In 1968, when he was a college freshman, Randy threw shot and discus for the freshman track team. After winning both events at the Long Beach State Relays, the varsity track coach approached him.

"Beck," he said, shaking Randy's hand, "I'm Coach P. You did a fine job here. Congratulations."

"Thank you, sir," Randy replied.

"I hope you plan to stick with the track program." Coach P. continued. "Varsity is tough you know, but you seem to have a lot of potential. Most of our throwers are considerably bigger than you. What do you weigh? Maybe 200 pounds?"

"At best," Randy admitted.

"That's small, Randy. Too small," the coach told him. "You can't fire sixteen inch guns from a destroyer. You've got to be a battleship."

"I've tried to bulk up," Randy said.

"Have you thought of taking steroids?" Coach P. asked.

Randy shook his head.

"The only way to be competitive is to use steroids. Everyone else is. Without 'em, you have no future as a college athlete. You'll just never keep up."

Coach P. looked at Randy for a long minute. "Well, what do you think?" he finally queried.

"I'm trying to get the whole picture," Randy answered, thinking out loud. "Steroids might help me in sports, and they might help the team, but do I care enough about that to risk the side effects?" He shook his head as if to clear away inner voices. "The answer is no," Randy said firmly. "If God wanted me to be a battleship, He would have made me a battleship."

Less Obvious Birds of Prey that Affect Friendships

Abusive Language and Swearing

What qualifies as swearing or abusive language? Words that degrade, humiliate, insult, or belittle others.

"Hey, wait!" you may say. "Swearing is everywhere."

True. Swearing is heard on playgrounds all over the country from the early grades and up. Many children grow up in homes where parents routinely swear at them and at each other.

"I don't know what to do anymore, Mrs. Beck," whispered the young voice on the other end of the line. "I came home from school and no one was home except the baby. He was standing up in his crib screaming. I changed and fed him and put him in the playpen. When Dad came home I told him that Mom had left Marly home alone again. Dad started swearing. He swore at Mom, who wasn't there. Then he swore at me because he could still smell the dirty diaper. I was thinking maybe I deserved a *thank you* for cleaning Marly up, but no, not from Dad. Then Mom arrived. They got into a huge fight. Mom blamed me for telling Dad she'd left. Why am I always the bad guy? By the time it was over I had to go to my room and convince myself that I AM NOT A S---HEAD. Or any of the other names they called me. I called my friend Leanne. I needed so badly to talk to someone. But Leanne sprinkles swear words through her conversation. She doesn't say them in anger or use them against me, but with so much of that garbage bouncing around my brain from my parents, it sounded ugly coming from Leanne. I got off the phone as soon as I could. I envy deaf people. Cussing is used around here so often that after every conversation I find myself bleeding."

This young woman moved in with neighbors shortly after this conversation. Although her parents claim to miss her and her mother whines about not having a babysitter, she has no plans to return home.

"I can't take care of them anymore," she told me recently. "I'm going to survive only if I stop putting up with people who abuse me with their words."

Sarcasm

Sarcasm is defined as *an ironical or scornful utterance; contemptuous and taunting language, and the use of cutting rebukes.*

Jordan once asked me why I, a sarcastic person, objected to it.

"How would you describe sarcasm, Jordan?" I asked him.

"It's *put-down humor*," he replied, "even though it's not funny."

"And when I put you down how do you feel?" I asked further.

"Like I have to defend myself by cutting you down, Mom." Jordan answered.

"Then what happens?" I asked.

"You say something else sarcastic. We get into a word fight. And usually I get really hurt."

"I hate it when I get sarcastic," I admitted. "I think I use sarcasm as a way to hide the urge to be violent. I'm really afraid there is an Incredible Hulk inside me. I know that's difficult to explain to you, son. Sarcasm is not a very good half-way measure but I want to change. Once I get started using it, it's usually too late for nice words. It's war."

"You know what else is bad, Mom?" Jordan asked. "When we get into a word war I spend the next few hours thinking awful thoughts so I can be ready for the next battle. When you come up to my room to apologize, it's hard to think forgiveness when my thoughts are still on revenge."

Humbling? You bet. Now that I've been given insight into the damage my sarcasm causes, what do I plan to do? Take a stand against the problem using the suggestions at the end of this chapter. If you ever chance to meet my Jordan, you might ask him how I'm doing!

Lying

"Who here is ready for the advanced slopes?" Randy asked the eager junior highers gathered around him on the youth group ski trip.

"I am!" shouted Will.

"I am!" yelled Kari.

"Okay, advanced skiers follow me. We'll warm up on the Shirley Lakes run. If that goes well, we'll hit the really advanced slopes. Everyone else report to Ginny over there. Let's go Will and Kari."

The three advanced skiers sat in silence on the chairlift to the top of the mountain. Will and Randy skied smoothly off the lift. Kari fell at the first turn. Will started down, bouncing over the moguls with ease. Kari pulled herself up, sidestepped over to Randy and fell at his feet.

"I'm not an advanced skier," she admitted. "I wanted the others to think I was really good at something. This is my second time ever on skis."

Randy looked down on the icy, mogul covered incline before them. "How do you intend to get down?" he asked her curiously.

"Can't I go back on the lift?" Kari asked.

"It's only for up. Down is against the rules." he replied. "You could try the run and see how you do," he suggested. "Even if you go down on your tush at least you'll be down."

"Forget it!" Kari exclaimed. "Too embarrassing! Could we ask the ski patrol to take me down?"

"Only after you fall and seriously hurt yourself," Randy answered drily. "The only other choice is to take your skis off and walk down."

"Not!" Kari cried. "If I do that, everyone will know I can't ski!"

Randy looked at Kari for a long time. His impulse was to give her a push and see what happened. Self-control got the better of him.

"Would you like to stay here and consider your options while I catch Will?" he asked. "You can give me your decision when I come up the lift again."

Kari bent over, undid her bindings, and stepped out of the skis. "You creep," she muttered. "You'd leave me up here to freeze while you enjoy yourself."

"It may seem easier to lie than to face reality," Randy commented mildly as he took off his skis. "If people are going to be able to trust you, they have to be able to believe what you say. What if you told me you were a great swimmer or horseback rider? Do you think I'd believe you after this?"

"But I am a good swimmer and an advanced horseback rider!" exclaimed Kari.

"Come on, Kari," Randy said with a sigh as he hoisted his skis to his shoulder. "It's a long walk down."

Why do people lie? It takes courage to admit problems and deal with them honestly. Young children lie because they see their parents or others getting away with it, or to avoid severe punishment. Abused children lie to protect themselves from the pain of the abuse. They may need professional or trained help to help them learn skills that will free them to face reality. Whatever the cause, telling lies very quickly becomes a threatening bird of prey that affects every area of life.

Bitterness

Bitterness comes from an unforgiving spirit that refuses to be healed and refuses to forgive and forget.

Motorcycles are not allowed in our neighborhood park. At various times, teenagers tempted by dirt paths and a grassy field ignore this rule. One particular afternoon I took Keidi and Nathan, who were toddlers, to the playground with the children of a Hmong refugee family our community was sponsoring.

The children's happy play was interrupted by the loud revving of two motorcycles as they swooped down the path right into the play area, scattering children everywhere. Everyone was screaming. The boys, who knew the rules, had come close to harming the children.

"Get out of here you guys!" I yelled savagely. "What's your problem? You know the rules. You could have killed someone."

The Hmong children disappeared into the bushes and headed home. The boys sneered at me as they roared off. I gathered up my kids and headed for the office where both of these boys' mothers worked.

"Your sons just about flattened the children playing at the park," I told them bitterly. "They tear around on those bikes with no consideration for others. Maybe they aren't responsible enough to own bikes like that," I suggested loudly.

"Maybe what you need is a dose of charity and understanding," one of the mother's told me through clenched teeth. "Maybe if they felt respected by meddlers like you their behavior would change for the better."

Shocked into silence, I turned and walked out.

But that wasn't the end of my anger. I took that incident home and brooded on it. Instead of forgiveness, bitterness grew in my heart. Even a passing glimpse of these women or their sons set my pulse racing in anger. Finally, I poured the whole problem out to my neighbor, Marilyn Hayes.

"Parents run into these things all the time. Your child breaks another child's new toy, or a neighbor's child pulls down and destroys your bird house," she told me. "I think the best thing to do is calmly express your feelings about what happened, have the involved parties make amends where needed, and then *let the little irritations roll off your back*. If these irritations become constant, or you feel wronged or offended in a larger way, *help* your friend by caring enough to confront him with the problem. If you need to wait for your anger to pass, then wait. Try to talk openly without attacking or embarrassing the other person."

She stopped and smiled at me. "I have one child who is super sensitive. If I don't balance criticism with large doses of affection my message is lost."

"Of course," she continued, "there's always the other side of the story. We have to let our friends respond to our comments and hear them out carefully.

Marilyn looked at me for a long moment. "Terry," she said, "this mother who responded so defensively probably felt attacked as a parent and is mad at you. If she should come and confront you with your response to her son's actions, will you be willing to listen to her? I ask you this because *yesterday this woman sat in that very chair and told me her side of the story.* She too struggles with bitterness. I hope you'll both avoid defensiveness and look for the truth in what is being said."

Jealousy

Jealousy, or resentful envy, is a problem all of us deal with at times. Jealousy keeps us from rejoicing in friends successes.

When appearances are important, we are jealous of those prettier or more stylish than us. When recognition is the focus, we are jealous of those who are given higher honors or are publicly thanked when we are not. When we are feeling unattractive, we are jealous of beautiful people. When we want to be cool but are not, cool people stir up envy. When wealth is important, we are jealous of rich people. And on and on and on.

Healthy contentment is the antidote to jealousy. This is summarized in the Serenity Prayer:

> *Lord, help me to accept the things I cannot change,*
> *to change the things I can,*
> *and the wisdom to know the difference.*

Harboring Birds of Prey Within Friendships

Shipley had a habit of teasing the weaknesses of others in the guise of being funny. His friend Jason was soon emulating him. In self defense, their friends avoided them both.

Friends who actively engage in bad habits together often alienate others. These habits can seem fun, but in the long run most friendships that are based on them erode.

Passive participation in bad habits is also a friendship poison.

Carlton never engaged in substance abuse, touched pornography or participated in illicit sexual activities. He was proud of his abstinence. Membership in his group at the high school demanded, however, that he go along with and support these destructive activities when done by his friends. He became the groups' *enabler* by covering for them when their behavior got them into trouble. Carlton called in sick for them when they were too hung over to get to school. He provided alibis or took the blame for some of their crimes.

Although Carlton avoided damaging his mind and body with substance abuse, he damaged his wholeness and integrity by lying and promoting the damaging habits of his friends. His kind of loyalty to his friends was not healthy.

Facing the Birds of Prey we are Harboring

Fortunately for all of us who find ourselves harboring bad habits, Chuck Swindoll, author of the book *Killing Giants, Pulling Thorns,* (Multnomah Press, 1978, page 67) has a five point plan for controlling them:

1. *Stop rationalizing.* We can become so hardened in our bad habits that we practice them without guilt. Instead of excusing our faults, we need to recognize them and work on abandoning them.

2. *Apply strategy.* Take one habit at a time. Set short-range and long-range goals. Learn to express anger constructively. Use physical barriers if possible (For example, remove all liquor from the house.) When necessary, get help from Alcoholics Anonymous, SmokEnders, professional counselors or others who can help you understand the real reasons for jealousy, sarcasm, bitterness, lying and other past mistakes. Then you will not be condemned to repeat them.

3. *Be realistic.* Don't let periodic failures cause you to give up. The American Cancer Society says that the more times a smoker tries to quit smoking, the more likely he is to be successful. If you blow it, don't give in to failure. Start trying to let go of those bad habits immediately.

4. *Be encouraged.* Enthusiasm strengthens self-discipline. We have tools available to help us control our problems. There are many programs and support groups available to help deal with the causes and heartbreak of living with birds of prey.

5. *Start today!* Don't procrastinate. The longer birds of prey are kept as pets, the bigger and more unmanageable they grow.

Remember. . .

Possession of one or more birds of prey moves us off the road to wholeness and maturity onto a detour of stagnation, selfishness, and deceit. Providing for an addiction, keeping it a secret, and attempting to function under its influence becomes the driving force of life. There is no time for others. Honesty loses priority to the needs of the growing birds. Healthy friendships vanish. Unhealthy friends stand by because they need company to share in their misery.

The moral of Joseph's story, which I try to pound into my children's heads, is that IT DOES NOT PAY TO DABBLE WITH DESTRUCTIVE THINGS. We have the skills that will help us stay out of trouble. Let's use them.

DISCUSSION QUESTIONS

1. List any birds of prey you may have picked up and are nourishing that may affect your ability to make and keep friends. (Look back to the Friendship Inventory in Chapter 2. How did you answer questions 41-46?)

   a) Where did the eggs come from? (Parents? Peers?)

   b) How do they affect friendships?

   c) How are you going to free yourself from them?

   d) How can you encourage wholeness in destructive areas that may be a part of your friendships?

intimacy \in't-e-me-se\ noun. *The state of belonging to or characterizing one's deepest or essential nature: marked by very close association, contact, or familiarity.*

Personal Intimacy— The Foundation for Intimate Friendships

When Betsy lived with us, she ran on the junior high track team. She did very well, qualifying first in both the 100 and 200 yard runs at the league championship meet. The 200 came first. She ran beautifully and won the gold medal. When the 100 came up, Betsy was nowhere to be found. The race went on without her and our school's runner took dead last.

"Betsy, you missed the 100 yard dash," Randy told her when she appeared. "Where were you?"

"Oh," Betsy replied calmly, "Nina didn't qualify for anything. Her friends begged me to let Nina run in my place. I'm trying to be friends with them so I told her she could run for me."

Our mouths dropped open. Fortunately, before we could insert our feet in them, the coach joined us.

"Betsy," he said angrily, "Nina told me you let her take your place and run in the 100. Why on earth did you do that? If you had run, the team probably would have gotten points for first place, and you would have been a double winner. Instead we're getting penalized for entering a non-qualified runner. Nina's pretty upset about that. If you really didn't want to run, you should have told me!"

"It wasn't that I didn't want to run," explained Betsy. "I just wanted to do something nice for Nina because she needed the encouragement and I'm trying to be her friend."

"Oh Betsy," the coach groaned. "I understand your reasons, but they were misguided. Next time talk to me before you do something like that, okay?"

Betsy had been eager for approval from Nina. To please her, she jeopardized the team's victory and pleased nobody.

Brian Kataptian was happily involved in the youth group at his church. The social activities, the Bible studies, the volunteer work in the community all gave him a sense of purpose and belonging. One day at school Brian overheard Tulsie, a girl he had a crush on, comment that she felt that the kids who participated in Brian's youth group were ingrown and snobby.

Brian quit attending youth group activities. He rationalized his behavior by saying he didn't want to be associated with ingrown and snobby people. However, he missed the fellowship and activities. Like Betsy, Brian ignored his true goals. He, too, gained nothing by his actions.

Several years ago I found myself bogged down by anger and depression. I couldn't figure out why. Randy and I were doing fine, the children were okay, but I just couldn't shake this cloud of gloom that seemed to follow me around. After weeks of living with this cloud, I began to wonder about my mental health. Then one day the postmaster showed me a list of twelve names he had attached to the back of our post office box.

"In the last fifteen months," he informed me, "these people all received mail in your box. Do they live with you or just used this box? Could I remove the list?"

When he said this, something deep inside of me went CLICK. He pinpointed the source of my depression. Yes, the individuals on this list all lived with us for various periods over the last months. The sheer numbers of them, the constant adjustments I made every time someone new joined the household, and the pressure I put on myself to accept these people into our home because we had room snowballed to the point of damaging my emotional health.

Personal Intimacy

Betsy, Brian and I suffered from lack of *personal intimacy.* This concept requires the knowledge of ones deepest goals and values, and the integrity to live life in accordance with them. Without personal intimacy we were unable to make decisions based on what we really thought or needed.

Because of this, Betsy became a *placater,* turning her desires and responsibilities over to others for the wrong reasons (approval by Nina.) Brian *did not recognize his own feelings, goals and values.* He became unduly influenced by the suggestions and discouragement of someone else. This caused him to make a decision that was not really what he wanted or believed. When this happened, he denied who he was and reduced himself to being a reflection of the thoughts and opinions of Tulsie.

I became a *minimizer,* conning myself into believing I could handle adjusting to many different people in our home all the time. "It isn't so bad," I told myself. "These people really need me." This was somewhat true, but, like Betsy and Brian, I was so eager to please that I had sidetracked the legitimate needs of my family and myself.

Who Am I? Is This the Person I Want to Be?

We cannot build strong, secure friendships without being in touch with our deepest selves. The goal of personal intimacy is to help us understand who we are and what direction we want for our lives. Once we learn this, we will be equipped to pursue intimacy with others.

Every day people assume many different roles. Big brother, little sister, son, daughter, student, team member, job holder, friend, playmate, partner—all of these are typical roles young people assume daily. Who they are within these roles may be influenced by other self-perceptions such as being a class clown, super student, cool kid, popularity queen, stud, good girl, dutiful son, antagonizing big sister, or bratty little brother.

How Do I Feel About Myself in the Roles I Play?

Step One of *The Personal Intimacy Inventory* at the end of this chapter will help define and evaluate how we feel about the roles we assume in our lives.

Examining how we feel about the roles we play can be difficult. We rarely think about relationships and emotions in this way. But knowing that our perception of reality is largely based on feelings, feelings obviously affect everything we do. Understanding this and working towards making interactions with people as healthy as possible is a major step towards understanding ourselves.

If I had examined my feelings about the role I was playing as landlady, hostess, and foster mother during the *dark cloud* period mentioned in the story at the beginning of this chapter, I would have been able to pinpoint my unfocused anger and grumpiness before my inner hostility levels boiled.

What Do I Value as a Person?

Values define who we are and how we behave. If friendships are valued, we will put time and energy into being a good friend. If good health is valued, we will pursue a healthy lifestyle. If value is given to a relationship with God, we will pursue godliness in every area of life. If we value honesty, integrity, kindness, loyalty, and justice, we will seek to live out these qualities. All of these are wholesome values.

On the negative side, if we value attracting attention to ourselves or being cool, we may choose to leave behind integrity and kindness to get people to notice us. If winning is important above all, we may choose to abandon fairness and good sportsmanship to be a continual winner. If escape from reality, feeling high, being part of the crowd, or expressing rebellious independence is valued, we may turn to drugs or alcohol.

Brian had to explore his deepest values in order to feel at peace about his decision to quit attending his youth group activities. Brian wanted to impress Tulsie, so he reacted to her critical comments without evaluating the truth of his own experience. Brian did not find the youth group to be ingrown or snobby. Once he understood the need to act on what he believed and not on someone else's opinion Brian felt free to rejoin the youth group. Thus he took a small step towards understanding and being true to his real self, not the one he had manufactured to please others.

Is My Current Behavior Getting Me the Results I Desire?

This question can often be the key to reordering areas of our lives that are unproductive and frustrating.

If we feel desparate for attention or popularity, but no one is responding to our attempts to be noticed, we can ask, "Is my current behavior getting me the results I desire?"

If work habits don't seem to yield our desired results, we can ask, "Is my current behavior getting me the results I desire?"

If our parents, spouses or friends don't listen to us or seem unaware of our feelings, we can ask, "Is my current way of relating to them getting me the results I desire?"

If we have an on going problem area of our lives, we can ask ourselves, "Is my current behavior getting me the results I desire?"

If, at any time the answer to these questions is *no*, then we need to seriously evaluate the problem and change our behavior to reach the goals we have set for ourselves. Too often we remain in unhealthy or unsatisfactory situations because we are comfortable in our routine and are unwilling to make the effort to change. We know ourself best when we have set personal goals and are working to accomplish them.

There are times when the basic need to survive, for our families and ourselves, deeply influences our ability to achieve our personal goals. This is something we rarely think of in our affluent society. When these situations arise, personal goals need to be set aside to meet the greater need of the family. When we have learned personal intimacy and know who we really are, we are able to respond to changes in our circumstances without panic or despair.

Jody desired to play varsity basketball and to be on the debate team in high school. However, when her father hurt his back and lost his job, Jody took a job after school to help support her family. She missed many school activities. As she realized how vital her contribution was to keeping the family together, Jody's priorities changed. She was able to adjust to the long hours of work and school more cheerfully.

Jody was called to support her deepest values, that of family survival, at a time when most teens are investing all of their resources in themselves. This is not the end of the story, however.

Jody called recently to talk over a new problem. Her Dad's back was healed. Her youngest brother was in school. Mom could get a job but neither parent was actively looking for work. The family survived on welfare and Jody's meager income.

"I cut short my childhood to help the family get on its feet," she told me sadly. "Now I have a chance to go to college in another state. Part of me wants to go, but part of me feels responsible to stay and keep helping the family financially."

"What are your goals for your family's finances?" I asked her.

"I'd like to see both my parents working and off welfare," she answered.

"Is your behavior getting you the results you desire?" I asked.

"What do you mean?" she questioned.

"What motivation do they have to get jobs and take care of themselves if you take care of them?" I queried.

"You're telling me my parents may not take action until they are forced to?" Jody probed.

"Look at it this way, Jody," I suggested. "Your actions got you the results you wanted while your parents couldn't work. You kept the family together. It was a loving sacrifice and I admire you for it. But now other factors come into play. You have felt needed and responsible in the role of caretaker and part of you is reluctant to give that up. Your parents felt safe and cared for by you and the welfare system, and part of them may be reluctant to give that up.

"You now have a chance to develop your own identity and interests. The family has an opportunity to stand on its own feet. Both of these are healthy choices, but you will have to let go of the old system. What is best for both you and the rest of your family? "

"You're right," Jody admitted. "I don't want to take care of them forever. It's been hard to set limits because the more I give, the more they seem to need. But if I don't set limits, I'll probably run away and not help with their real needs because I don't know how to handle my resentment and guilt."

Jody left for college the following month. Her father went back to school and her mother found a job working in a delicatessen. The family still struggles financially but they have what they need. The last time we spoke Jody told me, "I realize now that I was working hard to make everyone else's job in the family easier and less stressful. But I was taking on much more than I could handle and I wasn't living my own life. Now I'm learning to stay in touch with my own needs so I'll be healthy and sane when I'm called on to be a giver. I feel like I'm able to enjoy being young and alive for the first time in years!"

How Do We Connect With Our Feelings?

To begin maintaining a realistic connection with our feelings, we need to take time to evaluate personal thoughts and reactions in various situations.

Keeping a journal helps identify struggles and triumphs. Expressing emotions on paper provides a record of the triggers that set off feelings, both positive and negative. This helps us decide how to deal with emotions that are causing problems. Blowing off steam on paper can also provide a *time out* for regrouping responses and reactions. This relieves the tendency to take out anger or frustration on others.

Clustering is another way to tap into feelings. When Nathan struggles with frustration, I encourage him to write *FRUSTRATION* on the center of a piece of paper and circle it. He then draws lines out from the circle like sun rays, and labels them with the causes of his frustrations. He might surround the circle with comments like:

> *Johnny borrowed a dollar and promised to repay it today.*
>
> *He didn't and I couldn't pay for lunch.*
>
> *I lost one of my gym shoes.*
>
> *Mitchell, the worst player in the school, was on my basketball team in P.E. today. He helped lose our game. Then he criticized every thing I did and laughed whenever I missed a shot. Part of me wanted to beat him up but he's littler than I am and wears glasses.*
>
> *I missed the bus and got home late.*
>
> *I had to do chores before I could play.*

Looking at this list, it's evident that most of Nathan's frustration comes from his encounter with Mitchell. The other items are irritating, but would probably be less so if Nathan hadn't felt attacked and belittled on the basketball court.

By identifying the primary cause of frustration, Nathan is able to put the other incidents into perspective. Expressing his anger at Mitchell on paper defuses his emotional overload and allows him to get on with his day without dragging all of the earlier, frustration-causing baggage with him.

ASSIGNMENT: PERSONAL INTIMACY INVENTORY

Sit down with paper and pen at a time when you can be alone for at least one half hour. Try to eliminate distractions (turn off the television, radio.) Think through the following questions carefully, and answer them as completely as you can.

The Hats We Wear, the Roles We Play

List as specifically as you can the roles in which you see yourself on a blank piece of paper. After each role listed, describe yourself in that role using at least three to four adjectives. Then put an S if you are satisfied with the direction that relationship is going or a U if you are unsatisfied. For example:

1. Spiritual seeker: struggling, thankful, questioning   **S**
2. Dad and Mom's son: distant, loving, respectful   **U**
3. Joe's little brother: adoring, respectful, distant   **S**
4. Student: P.E. and math star, science humdrum, English dummy, teacher pleaser, try to act smarter than I feel   **S/U**
5. Tom's friend: leader in relationship, enjoy him but feel like the primary giver   **U**

If you are unsatisfied with any of the roles you've listed, take a few minutes to jot down the problems you perceive and what you can do to help change the relationships for the better.

What Are My Goals?

Setting realistic and flexible goals can provide a framework for growth. When Keidi was twelve, she and I went away for a Coming of Age Weekend. At that time, we talked about setting goals for herself in the next years. Here's a sampling from her list:

Physical Goals

> To get my Red Cross Lifeguard Training Certificate.
>
> To get my driver's license.
>
> To learn to sew and cook.
>
> To graduate from high school and college.

Spiritual Goals

> To read and study the Bible.
>
> To love others through friendship, inspiration, and encouragement.
>
> To learn healthy compassion.

Emotional Goals

> To learn to be myself and not what others want me to be.
>
> To be able to listen to other people's problems and attitudes without taking them on as my own.
>
> To write poetry.

Now It's Your Turn: *Personal Goals*

1. What physical goals do I want to reach this year?

    In five years?

    In ten years?

    What are the most important steps I will take to reach my physical goals?

2. What spiritual goals do I want to reach this year?

    In five years?

    In ten years?

    What are the most important steps I will take to reach my spiritual goals?

3. What emotional goals do I want to reach this year?

   In five years?

   In ten years?

   What are the most important steps I will take to reach my emotional goals?

4. Is my current behavior helping me reach my goals? If not, how can I change my behavior to move towards the results I desire?

A friend loves at all times.
--Proverbs 17:17

Intimate Friendships— Rare Treasures

Once we have an understanding of personal intimacy and are pursuing it in our lives, we can combine this knowledge with the friendship skills we have learned. Then we begin working towards enhancing the commitment, care and communication we offer our friends. While we do this, we can successfully face weaknesses and utilize our strengths, moving us towards wholeness at a faster pace.

Take the Risk of Knowing and Being Known

Kern lived three blocks away from my childhood home. We met in fourth grade. We discovered an abandoned tree fort at a friend's new house. Kern and I were the only ones daring enough to shimmy up the tree and test out the fort's rotted flooring. We suffered terribly from poison oak after that adventure. Misery bonded us into a unique friendship.

My memories of Kern are golden. He was the first boy ever to ask me to dance at a junior high sock hop. Together we spearheaded the campaign to allow girls to wear pants to school. When I was confused about social pressures or popularity issues, Kern always had a listening ear and comforting words to offer. He never seemed bothered by the fact that I was a head taller than he, or that I was female and he male. He treated me with respect and interest that was difficult for many boys that age. I loved him for it.

Kern was student body president, an honors student, and an outstanding soccer player. Our class voted him *Most Likely to Succeed*. He was the brightest and best of all of us, and we knew he would do great things with his life.

Kern committed suicide during our junior year in college. Even now, twenty years later, grief for him pierces my heart like a sword. Regrets wash over me. I never knew he was depressed or struggling.

At our fifth class reunion, my classmates and I talked sadly about Kern. Bruce, one of the class leaders, summed up our feelings when he said, "We were his friends and he gave a lot to each of us. Only now, looking back, do I see that Kern never shared *himself*. I knew there were problems he covered up. I keep thinking that if Kern could have shared his pain, someone could have helped him. I think he thought we'd love him only if he was perfect. I wish I'd seen how one-sided our friendship was. As close as we were, I really didn't know Kern at all."

When seeking intimacy in friendships, *take the risk of knowing and being known*. It is natural to want others to like us. In doing this, we tend to put on masks to hide our personal problems. To know others we must take off these masks. We need to be vulnerable, to struggle in each other's presence, to accept each other's weaknesses, and to reveal our true selves. When seeking intimacy, the key is to look for meaningful friends who are willing to know and accept the real you, and to be known themselves. We need to pursue people who can admit that they are not always successful or perfect. By accepting their own limitations, they will be able to accept imperfection in others.

To encourage sharing at a personal level, ask your friends thought-provoking questions that will reveal their dreams, struggles, and victories. Questions such as:

If time, money, and circumstances were not considerations, what would you do differently in life?

If you won $100,000, what would you do with it? With a million dollars? With five million?

Describe your dream house... dream car... dream job...

If you were another Mother Teresa of India, who would you help? How would you do it?

What is the greatest honor you have ever received? What honor would you most like to receive in the next five years?

What was the best day of your life? The worst?

If you could change something about yourself, what would it be? Why?

What do/did you like best about growing up in your family? What do/did you like least?

Spend Time Together

The summer I graduated from high school, I took a thirty-six day wilderness course with The National Outdoor Leadership School in the Wind River Mountains of Wyoming. My tent mate and climbing partner was Ann, a petite eighteen year old from a small town in the Midwest. Ann's background was vastly different from mine, but we hit it off from the first day. She was a better mountaineer than I and a constant source of encouragement when the trail climbed endlessly or the mosquitoes threatened to drive me crazy. Ann and I spent almost every minute together. I soon knew how often she washed her hair and what kind of toothpaste she preferred. She was the only one I trusted to guard the latrine entrance for me or to unsnag my fishing line. We quickly became close friends.

Exploring the high country was a good background for sharing our lives. Ann and I talked about everything. We climbed a large boulder to squint at the moon on the night the first Americans landed there. We learned teamwork in setting up camp and cooking our meals. I learned to trust little Ann with my life as I went *on belay* while rock climbing. Our home lives, our future goals, all became secondary to the intimacy that developed between us as we faced new adventures and difficult challenges together.

The course ended at a hotel in Lander. Sadly, so did our friendship.

We said tearful good-byes. Ann donned her leather pants and jacket and rode her motorcycle home. She looked forward to a job and marriage. I was heading for a year in Germany and then college. Although we'd promised to write, the experiences we'd shared were not enough to span the distances, both physical and emotional, offered by our real lives.

My summer with Ann taught me that *true intimacy needs more than just one kind of shared experience. We need to see each other in a variety of settings and circumstances.*

Living in Germany was another isolated experience for me. Having learned more about the requirements of intimacy, I worked harder at getting to know my roommate, Marcia. We talked whenever we were together. I tried at every opportunity to explore Marcia's life and invite her into mine. It was Marcia's idea to help with the grape harvest, attend huge parties put on by local brewers, visit famous landmarks, and sing in a local choir. Sightseeing on rented bikes, jogging, and learning German folk dancing were my ideas.

We didn't mesh perfectly in every area. Marcia had a steady boyfriend. She spent many weekends visiting Heinz. I tried to keep up with their adventures by listening to the tales Marcia brought home, encouraging her to share an area of her life in which I couldn't participate. And I tried to get to know Heinz, even though, at the time, his English was as limited as my German.

Marcia and I agreed to study each other's lives. I learned Marcia's likes and dislikes and she mine. We sent home for books that made an impact on our lives and read them together. We talked. I didn't understand everything Marcia enjoyed, but in seeking to understand or agreeing to peacefully disagree we opened the door for intimacy.

As we became aware of what was going on in each other's life, our friendship deepened. I realized that intimate friends are people with whom we have learned to share our deepest feelings, hopes, and needs. By the end of the year, Marcia was the most intimate friend I'd ever had. This time, the story didn't end when we parted. We finished college. She married Heinz and I married Randy. We are both raising large families in California. We write regularly. When we visit, the years roll away and we share our hearts. The investment we made in our friendship twenty-five years ago still bears precious fruit today.

Keep Friendship a Priority Through Giving

When Susan came to live with us, she came with a $600 phone bill. Her mother was dead. Her father was a permanent resident in a VA hospital. Older brothers were raising her. The high phone bill came from desperate attempts to call Dad (person to person) and inform him of the abuse she was suffering at home. The hospital phone was in the hall. By the time Dad was lifted out of bed, put in a wheelchair and wheeled to the phone, Susan owed the phone company big time.

Susan fit into our family happily. In some areas she was mature and capable. In others, she was way behind her sixteen years. Emotionally she was starving. I held her on my lap like a baby and rocked her as we talked. It was a kind of caring she'd longed for but never received. Like a sponge, Susan absorbed all the love we had to give. There were days when we felt sucked dry. But our energy to give was constantly renewed by Susan's positive response. She didn't hoard our love; she responded by reaching out and loving others.

Susan grew up and moved into her own apartment. We were still the ones she called on for help with problems or for advice. We brought her groceries when she was broke and encouraged her to start her own business. She married. She had two children. I pictured my friendship with Susan as one where she leaned on me. It was limited by that one-sidedness, but, like a parent with a child, I accepted that. Then our friendship changed.

Our baby, Jordan, had to have emergency surgery. Randy assumed I could handle the waiting room scene by myself. I thought so too, until the gurney carrying Jordan was wheeled into the operating room. Alone and terrified, I fell apart. Around the corner came Susan. She'd brought Kleenex, a book of jokes for distraction, and her love and support.

"I knew you couldn't go through this on your own, Terry," she said. "When Randy told me you were alone, I traded shifts with a friend at work so I could come and sit with you."

From that point on our friendship grew dramatically. Thinking back over the last years, I saw how Susan had been giving to me—of her gift of listening, her laughter, her wisdom, and her caring for my family. Although she still occasionally calls me *Mom*, what had once been one-sided was now balanced, and to this day we refer to ourselves as *forever friends*. We kept a growing friendship alive by giving; we were rewarded with intimacy.

Work Through Hard Times

Roger was a regular around our house during my oldest brother Michael's high school years. He was an only child and loved the hustle and bustle of the Allen household. He also loved food. Mom would often find him sitting on a chair with his head inside our refrigerator gazing longingly at the leftovers stored inside.

"What are you doing, sitting here with the refrigerator door wide open, Roger?" Mom asked the first time she caught him.

"It's beautiful," Roger told Mom, smacking his lips. "My parents are never home. Our refrigerator is full of Sara Lee. When I look at all this homemade food, a real feeling of family washes over me."

Michael often teased Roger, telling him that the only reason they became friends was because of Roger's availability—every time Michael turned around, Roger was at our house. Perhaps because Roger did enter the rhythm of Michael's life, the boys became good friends. Michael talked about everything and anything with Roger, and Roger poured his heart out to Michael.

Then Roger's mother disappeared. Roger and his father went through two weeks of agony, including missing persons reports and police searches. Finally a postcard from Mexico let them know that she was safe, getting a divorce, and planning to marry another man.

Roger flipped. His visits to our house were punctuated with long periods of stony silence alternated with outbursts of rage against his mother. When those feelings faded, he took a very anti-women stance on all issues. He argued about everything and wasn't much fun to have around. He was especially rude to Mom and Michael found himself irritated with Roger to the point of not wanting to let him in the house.

"I understand how you feel," Mom told Michael as they talked over the problem. "But we are Roger's anchor right now. You miss your friendship with Roger and you want to protect me. We've enjoyed having Roger as part of our lives, and he has been very important to you as a friend, right?"

"Right," Michael answered.

"Roger is going through the normal stages of grief. He needs a safe place to do that. If Roger's anger becomes harmful to you or me or the other children, we'll have to ask him to go elsewhere. I will talk to him about his behavior in our home. He really doesn't see beyond his own feelings. I know it would hurt him to lose us right now."

"But having him here is like inviting a rain cloud into the house," Michael told her.

"You're right," Mom said with an understanding smile. "And he's your friend. You get rained on more than the rest of us. If you need to ask him to stay away, you should. But I am encouraging you to not give up during this rough time. Roger will get through this. When your Uncle Harold first started working as an engineer on ferry boats in Puget Sound, he used to come home after big storms completely exhausted. When Betty Ann fussed about his work, he reminded her that '*smooth seas never made a good sailor.*' I've often applied that to friendships that were struggling."

Michael hung on through several long months of Roger's pain. Then the sun rose again in Roger's life. Michael rejoiced. He and Roger learned that working through problems, comforting grief, enduring losses, or surviving failures are the kinds of emotional gifts friends may be called upon to give in the pursuit of intimacy.

Take the Initiative Yourself

A young woman at a friendship seminar told me that she longed for intimacy in friendships. When I asked her what steps she was taking to see those friendships happen, she was surprised.

"I've never even thought about taking steps," she told me honestly. "I guess I thought that if intimacy was meant to happen, it would happen. I have lots of good friends, but none of them are intimate. What can I do to help things along?"

Building on suggestions from the audience, we came up with these *Intimacy Initiating Ideas:*

1. *Make a list of your meaningful friends. With which of these people do you desire to become more intimate?*

2. *To deepen these relationships, look for opportunities to draw these friends out, to spend more personal time with them, to serve and encourage them. Get the ball rolling by being the giver.*

3. *Don't be afraid to express your feelings. Words like, "Dana, our friendship is really important to me. I enjoy the time we spend together and I hope you feel the same. If you are interested, I'd like to make a commitment to work together more this year," can open doors of mutual effort towards intimacy.*

4. *Ask yourself: Is my current behavior encouraging intimacy in my friendships? If not, how can I change my behavior to make me the kind of friend I would like to have?*

5. *Look for ways to reach out and minister to other people with your friend. Volunteer work, teaching Sunday school, visiting shut-ins; these activities offer unusual insight and appreciation of a friend's character, strengths and weaknesses.*

Keep Trying

When a friendship stalls just as you hoped it was headed towards intimacy, evaluate the problem and try again, either with the same friend or with a different one. If we practice the skills of friendship in relationships, we set the stage for intimacy. However, intimacy cannot be forced. It will happen when personalities, attitudes and circumstances permit.

Remember. . .

Intimacy involves growing closer in understanding, compassion, commitment, and caring for another person. Working with friends to survive the storms of life builds trust, acceptance, and loyalty. This is the essence of intimacy.

ASSIGNMENT:

a. List your closest friends. After each friend's name, answer the following questions.

— Are we wearing masks or being real with each other? What can we do to make needed changes?

— Are we willing to invest time in the relationship?

— Are we making this friendship a priority through giving?

— Can we work through hard times together?

— Am I harboring a bird of prey that is or will impair our friendship? What is it and how can I work toward eliminating the problem? (What can I do? What help can I ask for from this friend?)

> *"...that moment one definitely commits oneself, then providence moves too. All sorts of things occur to help one that would never otherwise have occurred. A whole stream of events issues from the decision, raising in one's favor all manner of unforeseen incidents and meetings and material assistance which no man could have dreamed would have come his way... Whatever you can do or dream you can, begin it. Boldness has genius, power and magic in it. Begin it now."*
>
> --Goethe

Conclusion

My sister and brother-in-law gave me their old computer when they upgraded their system. The following week we sold our antiquated typewriter for five dollars and I began molding the material from *The Workshop on Friendship* into book form. My sister also gave me the above quote from Goethe. The two gifts worked hand in hand. Divine providence moved and I wrote. Not only did help in the form of encouragement, technical advice, and research articles pour in from sources all over the country, but all manner of unforeseen incidents and meetings came my way.

Writing about friendship has been inspiring, enlightening (as to the condition of my own heart), and sometimes painful. I have had to relearn these skills at levels that were at times both surprising and uncomfortable. "Shouldn't someone who teaches friendship skills to others sail smoothly through her own relationships?" I ask myself. It doesn't seem to work that way. The mastery of skills does not occur overnight. Just as I think I've arrived at a new level of understanding, a new challenge appears. Success and struggle travel hand-in-hand.

This may be your experience also—don't be discouraged. You are beginning a journey that aligns itself with the will of God—that we should love our neighbors as ourselves. With this foundation, Divine providence moves. We do not travel alone. Encouragers, helpers, comforters, advisors and supporters will pass our way. We call these messengers our friends. They are the priceless treasures of the heart.

This is what I wish for you.

Terry Beck

Note to Readers:

The author is collecting ALL-STAR FRIENDSHIP stories for possible future publication. If you have an encouraging friendship story that you would like to share and perhaps see in print, please write it out in as much detail as you can (time, place, people involved, ages of those people and their relationship to you) and send it to:

Terry Beck
P.O. Box 91
Mount Hermon, CA 95041

Appendix A

Age Appropriate Reading on Friendship Problems and Triumphs

I often hear educators and family counselors remark that children absorb new information and skills most readily if we can catch them at *teachable moments*. Waiting until children are ready to listen before we zap them with important information or lessons seems reasonable to me. It isn't as easy as it sounds. Randy and I juggle full schedules. Our children range from kindergarten to college. Their activities rarely happen at the same time or in the same place. Carpooling alone inspires thoughts of hara-kiri. Teachable moments around our house usually have to be helped along a bit.

To facilitate teachable moments, I read books aloud to my younger children and I try to read the same books my teenagers are reading. Books that talk about friendship offer an opportunity to identify and discuss friendship dynamics. Each story can generate *who? what? when? where? why?* and *how did they feel?* questions about friendship struggles and triumphs.

Take the book *FROG AND TOAD ARE FRIENDS* listed in this Appendix for 2-4 year olds. In the last story of the book, Toad is sad because he never gets mail. Frog runs home, writes his friend a letter which verbally affirms their friendship and mails it. He then runs back to wait for the mail carrier (a snail) with Toad.

After reading this aloud to Ben and Laurel I might ask them, "Can you tell me the main idea of this story?" (Toad is sad. His friend Frog wants to cheer him up.)

"Why was Toad sad?" (He didn't ever get mail.)

"Why did Toad want mail?" (Because mail makes you feel special.)

"What did Frog do to personally love Toad?" (First he told Toad he understood his feelings and then he ran home and wrote Frog a letter and sent it in the mail.)

"How did Toad feel about that?" (He felt happy because Frog wrote that he was glad he and Toad were good friends and Toad got a letter.)

"Do you feel good when your friends tell you how special you are to them?" (Yes.)

"How will your friends feel if you tell them how much they mean to you? (They will feel good and happy about being my friend.)

"Can you think of someone who might be happy to get a letter in the mail telling them how loved they are?" ("Me!" Laurel and Ben both reply.)

"I know," Laurel tells us, "I could write Ben a letter and he could draw me a picture and we could send them to each other..."

Keidi and I read *WHO WALK ALONE* (on the 14-18 year old list) simultaneously. This is the story of Ned Ferguson, an American who contracted leprosy while stationed in the Philippines during the Spanish-American War (1898.) Once diagnosed, Ned gave up life as he knew it and moved to Culion, an island set aside for lepers in the Philippines. For the next twenty-five years, through struggle and challenges he built a life for himself while bringing leadership, dignity, and hope to his fellow lepers.

Keidi and I discussed the faith that gave Ned strength to overcome his despair and live without self-pity or anger. The love, giving and joy that Ned gave to others on Culion inspired us both.

We wondered how we might react in Ned's shoes. Keidi expressed concern about the endurance of her own ability to set aside self-pity and make life better for those around her. "It boils down to faith," she told me, "Faith in God and faith in myself. Could I maintain Ned's level of faith day after day, year after year, far away from my family and shunned by the healthy world?" We talked of ways to build a spiritual reservoir to take us through troubled times. While we didn't specifically cover the who-what-when-where-why-how format, we shared in depth our impressions and feelings about the book. It was a teachable moment for both of us.

Nathan and I sometimes make a game of thinking up questions for each other regarding who used this or that skill most successfully or failed most dismally in a particular book. We talk about feelings—how did the character feel after being treated as he was treated? Was there a better choice of action for the characters? How would you feel in a struggling character's place?

When possible, I target virtues my child has displayed as positive examples. In a discussion with Jordan I might say, "That guy really worked hard, didn't he? You are a good worker Jordan. You could meet that kind of a challenge if you had to."

After each book listed, I have noted a few of the friendship qualities or problems the story presents to help you reinforce a friendship skill you are working on with your child. These books are meant to get you started. There are hundreds of books that deal directly with friendship-related skills. Discussions like these can also take place after appropriate television shows or movies.

As children learn to evaluate and sort out their own experiences and in those of book or movie characters, their perception of how they want to treat others and be treated themselves is clarified. This is an important step in loving others from the inside out.

2-5 Year Olds

Berenstain, Stan and Jan. *TROUBLE WITH FRIENDS* (compromise)

Cameron, Ann. *THE STORIES JULIAN TELLS* (honesty)

Carrick, Carol. *WHAT A WIMP!* (dealing with bullies)

Dalgliesh, Alice. *THE COURAGE OF SARAH NOBLE* (courage)

De La Mare, Walter. *MOLLY WUPPIE* (courage, giving, responsibility)

Gaeddert, LouAnn. *NOISY NANCY NORRIS* (courtesy)

Lasker, Joe. *HE'S MY BROTHER* (patience, giving, understanding, compassion)

Lobel, Arnold. *FROG AND TOAD ARE FRIENDS* (cheerfulness, affirmation, caring, personal loving, helpfulness, teasing)

Marshall, James. *GEORGE AND MARTHA RISE AND SHINE, GEORGE AND MARTHA ENCORE* (both books—kindness, honor, affirmation, personal loving, compassion)

Robinet, Harriette. *RIDE THE RED CYCLE* (courage, encouragement)

Sura, Mary. *CHESTER* (overcoming prejudice, jealousy, unkindness)

Zemach, Margot. *TO HILDA FOR HELPING* (giving, jealousy)

6-8 Year Olds

Brown, Marc. *THE TRUE FRANCINE* (honesty, true character)

Dahl, Roald. *CHARLIE AND THE CHOCOLATE FACTORY* (courtesy, kindness, giving)

Fox, Mem. *WILFRID GORDON MCDONALD PARTRIDGE* (giving)

Hurwitz, Johanna. *ALDO APPLESAUCE* (making new friends)

Killilea, Marie. *KAREN* (giving, cheerfulness, appreciation, overcoming handicaps)

MacLachlan, Patricia. *SARAH PLAIN AND TALL* (acceptance, caring, giving)

Slote, Alfred. *LOVE AND TENNIS* (inner values, wholeness)

Smith, Janice Lee. *THE KID NEXT DOOR AND OTHER HEAD-ACHES* (ups and downs of friendships, working through problems, forgiveness)

9-12 Year Olds

Byars, Betsy. *THE SUMMER OF THE SWANS* (giving)

Gallico, Paul. *THE SNOW GOOSE* (giving, courage, recognizing healthy standards, sacrifice)

Gleeson, Libby. *I AM SUSANNAH* (losing friends, making friends)

L'Engle, Madeleine. *A WRINKLE IN TIME* (loyalty, love, personal intimacy)

Lewis, C.S. *THE LION, THE WITCH, AND THE WARDROBE* (all ages -honesty, courage, integrity, kindness)

Patterson, Katherine. *BRIDGE TO TERABITHIA* (friendship, grief)

Pevsner, Stella. *AND YOU GIVE ME A PAIN, ELAINE* (conflict in relationships, kindness, giving)

Sachs, Marilyn. *WHAT MY SISTER REMEMBERED.* (loyalty, forgiveness, courage)

Simon, Norma. *HOW DO I FEEL?* (resolving conflict, jealousy)

Voight, Cynthia. *DICEY'S SONG* (responsibility, sacrifice, courage, giving, honesty)

Wrightson, Patricia. *THE SUGAR GUM TREE* (dealing with conflict in friendships)

11-14 Year Olds

Adler, Carole. *ALWAYS AND FOREVER* (prejudice, fear, loyalty, commitment)

Cleaver, Vera and Bill. *WHERE THE LILIES BLOOM* (giving, unkindness, encouraging each other to wholeness)

Kerr, M.E. *THE SON OF SOMEONE FAMOUS* (strangers becoming friends)

Mazer, Norma Fox. *MRS FISH, APE, AND ME, THE DUMP QUEEN* (cruelty, expectations, snobbery, giving)

Sayers, Gale. *I AM THIRD* (friendship, compassion, giving)

Sebestyen, Ouida. *WORDS BY HEART* (encouraging each other to wholeness, prejudice, faith, giving, dealing with difficult people)

Voight, Cynthia. *SONS FROM AFAR* (loyalty, tolerance, forgiveness, personal intimacy)

14-18 Year Olds

Burgess, Perry. *WHO WALK ALONE* (faith, giving, encouraging to wholeness)

Bush, Alice *HE WILL NOT WALK WITH ME* (hero worship, recognizing true friendship qualities)

Butler, Beverly. *LIGHT A SINGLE CANDLE* (being different, courage, giving, personal intimacy)

Craven, Margaret. *I HEARD THE OWL CALL MY NAME* (compassion, giving, faith, encouraging to wholeness)

Greene, Bette. *SUMMER OF MY GERMAN SOLDIER* (integrity, dealing with irregular people, loyalty)

Hautzig, Esther. *THE ENDLESS STEPPE* (flexibility, change, hardship, courage, faith, unfairness)

Kotlowitz, Alex. *THERE ARE NO CHILDREN HERE.* (giving, courage, loyalty, forces that shape friendships in difficult situations)

Potok, Chaim. *THE CHOSEN* (overcoming cultural differences, loyalty)

OTHER FINE BOOKS FROM R&E ! ! !

BUILDING HEALTHY FRIENDSHIPS:Teaching Friendship Skills To Young People by Terry A. Beck. Using anecdotes, humor, and her unique personal experience, Terry Beck offers a step-by-step approach for helping young people of all ages learn essential friendship skills at home or in the classroom These skills can help children to establish healthy relationships throughout their lives. Parents, educators, and the young may use this practical guide in small group settings or on an individual basis.

$9.95	ISBN 1-56875-073-0
Soft Cover	Order #073-0

THE ABCs OF PARENTING: Keep Your Kids in Touch and Out of Trouble by Joan Barbuto. Raising children in our society is more difficult than ever before. This book gives parents the practical tools they need to raise responsible, capable and well-adjusted children. It teaches parents the 20 rules of discipline they must know and apply and how to avoid the types of discipline that are ineffective and psychologically damaging.

$14.95	ISBN 1-56875-062-5
Soft Cover	Order #062-5

WHAT IS HAPPENING TO OUR CHILDREN: How to Raise them Right by Mardel Gustafson. Here is a book that will help parents to restore some old-fashioned values in our children. It is time, the author believes, for women to return to the most important job of all—raising their children. Only in this way will the strength of the family be restored. With this stronger parental influence, children can be taught the values that will make them responsible citizens and have the strength to stay off of drugs and alcohol. Written by a former teacher and Sunday school instructor.

$7.95	ISBN 1-56875-044-7	Order #044-7

SURVIVING SUMMERS WITH KIDS: Fun Filled Activities for All by Rita B. Herron. It comes every year, inexorably like death and taxes, the dreaded summer break. When schools close, parents are at the mercy of their unoccupied and restless children. This light-hearted, easy-to-read book is filled with anecdotes and tips for surviving summer vacations with your psyche intact. Written by a teacher and mother.

$9.95	ISBN 1-56875-052-8
Soft Cover	Order #052-8

TALKING JUSTICE: 602 Ways to Build & Promote Racial Harmony by Tamera Trotter & Jocelyn Allen. It is said that a journey of a thousand miles begins with a single step. This important new book is a map to the small steps that each of us can take on the path to ending prejudice and hatred. We can use these methods to bridge the gap that exists between us and members of other races. With each small, tenuous action we take, we are that much closer to understanding each other. This simple yet profound guide is ideal for teachers, clergy and individuals who want to end the hatred and venture into a strange, but beautiful new land of harmony and cooperation.

$6.95	ISBN 0-88247-982-2
Soft Cover	Order #982-2

BECOMING THE ME I WANT TO BE: A Self-Help Guide to Building Self-Esteem by Don G. Simmermacher. Everything that you do in life, from the amount of money you make to the person you marry, is determined by your self-esteem and self-image. It is believed that most of us use less than 10% of our true potential, and that if we learned how to tap into it we could transform our lives. This book will help you discover and develop a more powerful sense of self to help change your life dramatically.

$9.95   ISBN 1-56875-055-2   Order #055-2

THE POWER OF POSITIVE EDUCATION by Will Clark. Our education system is failing our children. It is not preparing them to succeed in a world which is growing increasingly more complex and demanding. Instead of helping children to become motivated learners, we are teaching them to be irresponsible and destructive. This book offers a new model and a new hope. It teaches parents, educators, political and business leaders how to work together to provide our children with the education they need and deserve.

$9.95   ISBN 1-56875-057-9   Order #057-9

THE WINNING FEELING by John R. Kearns & Garry Shulman. Most children idolize athletes. Now, there is a book that teaches how to apply the success for techniques of world class athletes toward academics. After spending years coaching some of the world's greatest athletes, and coaching their coaches, the authors have created a program that teaches students of all ages to become winners in the classroom. The authors have conducted over 300 workshops on enhancing self-esteem, the essential element in all success. Their "Winning Feeling" program has been successfully implemented in Canadian classrooms for four years.

$9.95   ISBN 1-56875-057-9   Order #057-9